ENDORSEMENTS

Master writer Steve Wohlberg has done it again. His new book, *Demons in Disguise*, reveals occultism's dark side, giving the reader chilling goose bumps which then become thrilling goose bumps when Steve portrays the final coming of the Holy One whom the unholy powers of evil fear the most. Virtual reality at its best, thoroughly scriptural, a fascinating read!

—Dave MacPherson
Author of *The Rapture Plot*
and *The Incredible Cover-up*

"Ye know not what you play with." A phrase I often tell those who think playing with the "other side" is some kind of a game. Steve Wohlberg hits the nail on the head with his new book, *Demons in Disguise*. Not only is this book well researched, but he also reveals Hollywood's fascination with romanticizing the dark side of the afterlife. We must take a more active stance in protecting not only our kids, but also understanding what many times is portrayed as safe.

Steve Wohlberg has provided a wonderful resource enabling us to actively seek out more "family-friendly" forms of entertainment."

—Dr. Rus D. Jeffrey
Author of *Frame by Frame: A Family-Friendly Guide to the Movies*
News Director for WACK 1420 AM, Newark, NY
Senior Pastor, Fresh-Wind Ministries

Wohlberg has begun a new acronym: D.I.D. (Demons In Disguise). Here is persuasive unmasking of the supernatural imposters from the other side! This gripping book has candidly documented why popular beliefs about the afterlife have made the world's masses vulnerable; even the mediums, channelers and Hollywood moviemakers are duped.

—Daniel Knauft
Author of *Search for the Immortal Soul*

Steve Wohlberg, following the tracks I forged with my book *The Mystery of Death*, shows how impersonating spirits can reach across to an entire generation through channelers, bestselling books, and countless television specials. Dark powers, masquerading as the deceased, are able to impact countless lives with occult beliefs. Using lucid insight from Scripture, Steve Wohlberg does a commendable job in revealing the hidden dynamics at work in this time of deception.

—Tal Brooke
Author of *The Mystery of Death*
President, Spiritual Counterfeits Project

What can be more fascinating than the idea of breaking through the ultimate barrier to the Great Beyond? Perhaps only this: to learn the truth about all such efforts and to discover that they are part of a plot of deception by the dark side of the supernatural! Steve Wohlberg has done his homework and presents his findings in this spellbinding new book that you will find difficult to put down. Best of all, he reveals the answer to the universal human longing for immortality that sends people to mediums, spiritualists and the like in the first place. I highly recommend *Demons in Disguise*.

—Edward William Fudge
Author of *The Fire That Consumes*

As we near the close of time, our invisible adversary is now pulling out all the stops in an effort to confuse and confound all humanity with counterfeit "power, signs, and lying wonders" (see 2 Thessalonians 2:9). The only way to avoid being deceived is to read and understand the Holy Word of God. I believe the Lord has raised Steve Wohlberg up and blessed him with the gift of teaching His Word in a clear and concise manner. In his new book, *Demons in Disguise*, Steve provides unquestionable proof that what may appear to be harmless, or even good, is often in reality a dangerous, deceptive trap of evil. *Demons in Disguise* is a must read for those who are seeking truth in a world awash with lies.

—Rob Pue
Publisher, *Wisconsin Christian News*

DEMONS IN DISGUISE

Steve Wohlberg

Destiny Image₀ Publishers, Inc.
P.O. Box 310
Shippensburg, PA 17257-0310

"Speaking to the Purposes of God for this Generation
and for the Generations to Come."

For Worldwide Distribution, Printed in the U.S.A.

ISBN 13: 978-0-7684-2491-1

This book and all other Destiny Image, Revival Press, MercyPlace, Fresh Bread, Destiny Image Fiction, and Treasure House books are available at Christian bookstores and distributors worldwide.

For a U.S. bookstore nearest you, call
1-800-722-6774.

For more information on foreign distributors, call
717-532-3040.

Or reach us on the Internet:
www.destinyimage.com

1 2 3 4 5 6 7 8 9 10 11 / 09 08 07

DEDICATION

This book is dedicated to the One who "was dead," but is "alive forevermore" (see Rev. 1:18).

CONTENTS

DEMON (noun):

—an evil spirit

—a source or agent of evil, harm, distress, or ruin

DISGUISE (transitive verb):

—to change the customary dress or appearance of

—to furnish with a false appearance or an assumed identity

FOREWORD

by Daniel Knauft

TIME magazine recently reported that 70 million Americans now believe in communication with the dead, which explains why Hollywood has seized upon the theme of the supernatural with movies and television shows such as *The Sixth Sense*, *Medium*, and *Ghost Whisperer*.

Do you know someone who has received a communication from the "other side"? Perhaps they received a message coming through one of the many current celebrity psychic mediums like John Edward or Allison DuBois, or even from a direct apparition of a deceased loved one. What did you think when you heard about their experience? Did it arouse your curiosity, or make you a believer in communication with the dead? If so, beware!

Recently I listened to psychic medium Steve Godfrey's radio talk show, *The Other Side*, which is broadcast coast to coast on Saturday nights. During this show, listeners call in, answer Godfrey's questions, and then wait for him to identify their dead relatives, talk with them, receive messages of advice and comfort, and then relay these messages to the listener. As I listened to one call-in after another, I couldn't help wondering, *On what basis are these callers evaluating this experience? How are they determining whether these not-of-this-world communications are really genuine? How do they know that the information relayed doesn't originate from an impostor—a demonic imperson-ator of a dead loved one?* It appears that millions of people, both religious and non-religious, are entirely ignorant of what the Bible teaches about necroman-cy, or communication with the dead.

Who are the ones most vulnerable to this emerging culture of the super-natural? First and foremost are those drawn by curiosity and entertainment, but are wholly unprepared to discern the true nature of the phenomenon. Second are those who do not believe the Bible's message of the unseen world, and who inhabits it. Third, there are those grieving the loss of a loved one, and who are therefore inclined to wish for comforting information from a deceased friend or family member.

If you find yourself in any of these categories, the book you now hold in your hands will prove to be a gripping, well-documented, incalculable bless-ing. No matter how this book has come to your attention, I urge you to read it from cover to cover. It will open your eyes, inform you about malicious, invisible forces, and above all, it will bring you into the tender arms of One who truly loves you, tasted death for you, and was raised from the dead.

Enjoy. Be warned, and enlightened!

—Daniel Knauft
Author of *Search for the Immortal Soul*

INTRODUCTION

Ghost encounters are happening every day to people everywhere, and the events prove that we are not alone. When people encounter what they perceive to be a ghost or spirit, their lives are forever changed. The ultimate question—Is there life after death?—has just been answered for them.

—Our Haunted Lives: True Life Ghost Encounters [1]

E VERYONE knows that death is real. Cemeteries speckled with silent tombstones dot cities, towns, and country sides across the globe. "The end of the story is: you die. We all die," declared Hollywood actor Michael J. Fox, who has Parkinson's disease. Fox was right. Death awaits us all—we just don't know when it will strike.

Obviously, no one wants his or her existence to culminate inside a casket beneath dirt. Therefore, as we face the prospect of our own eventual funeral, it's only natural that we long for some kind of comforting assurance of an immortal existence "beyond the grave." *Is there life after death?* We all hope so. This remains the most pondered question of all time.

Perhaps you haven't noticed the phenomenon, but vast numbers have recently become convinced that there is indeed a happy existence beyond death's door. Their belief is based on something highly unusual, yet hard to ignore: Surprisingly, they've met a ghost. Yes, you read that right, *a ghost*. In spite of scientific skepticism, belief in the afterlife is surging, and one big reason is because the spirits of dead people are apparently talking from the Other Side. Thanks to NBC, CBS, Disney, and Discovery Channel, communication with spirits is being promoted right on TV. Millions are watching, and believing.

It's true, many mediums, clairvoyants, and psychics who claim to have had personal conversations with your deceased Uncle Bob or Aunt Sue are nothing more than unscrupulous con artists preying on the naïve and gullible. They're a dime a dozen and will do anything to deplete their victim's bank accounts. But is the entire notion of an invisible realm only wishful thinking? Countless skeptics used to think so, until they became convinced otherwise by encountering real spirits. Now they know better. In the following pages you will discover bona fide examples of real spirits making real contact with real people. The spiritual world isn't imaginary. It exists. I'll prove it.

As we embark on this fascinating journey, let me clarify that I, Steve Wohlberg, am a firm believer in life after death. I'm not an atheist, agnostic, or skeptic. I believe in an exciting hope that penetrates the tomb, and in the strong possibility of becoming eternally reunited with our deceased friends and loved ones. My faith is based, not on the opinions of so-called "experts," scholars, best-selling authors, talk show personalities (either preachers or mediums), nor on a personal experience with a ghost; instead, it's deeply rooted in the plain teaching of the world's most widely read book. I'm not talking about the *Harry Potter* novels, but the Holy Bible.

You are about to discover credible evidence that an unseen world exists, and that it is inhabited by a vast network of highly intelligent personalities. But here's the catch. Not all of these invisible entities are friendly, even though they may claim to be. On the contrary, vast numbers are consummate tricksters, with thousands of years of experience in the art of distortion. The Bible's last book, called "The Revelation," lifts the veil and exposes the true nature of these pretenders, their methods of working and apocalyptic goals. Notice carefully:

> ***For they are spirits of demons,*** *performing signs, which go out to the kings of the earth and of the whole world, to gather them to the battle of that great day of God Almighty. ... And they gathered them together to the place called in Hebrew, Armageddon* (Revelation 16:14, 16, emphasis added).

This is a prophecy. It predicts a global movement of deception carefully orchestrated to delude the entire world before the biblical battle of Armageddon. According to "The Revelation," the invisible coordinators of this end-time tsunami are calculating masterminds identified as "spirits of demons." Based on current events, I am convinced that Revelation's prophecy is in the process of fulfillment, and that Hollywood is ignorantly helping to make it happen.

Demons in Disguise will help protect you from being ensnared.

ENDNOTE

1. Jeff Belanger, *Our Haunted Lives: True Life Ghost Encounters* (Franklin Lakes, NJ: Career Press, Inc., July 2006), publisher comments. See http://search.barnesandnoble.com/booksearch/isbninquiry.asp?ean=9781564148568&z=y#PUB.

Chapter 1

HOLLYWOOD GHOSTS

I am a medium and profiler. This means I can predict future events. I can get into a person's mind, I can detect health problems in people, and I can communicate with the dead. Yes, I see dead people.

—Allison DuBois, best-selling author, professional medium [1]

"WHAT is it with the dearly departed? Seems they're everywhere lately," reported an unnamed author in *People* magazine. "Ghosts, ghouls and spirits are invading prime time."[2] So began an eerie article entitled, "They See Dead People," which not only recounted Hollywood's current fascination with story lines featuring close encounters with spirits, but which also showcased three individuals—Tom Murdic (Franklin, TN), Kristin Jorgensen (Oxford, MI), and Rhonda Witter (Orangevale, CA)— who say they "live with friendly ghosts." Before exploring these and other incidents involving otherworldly visitors, let's talk about TV.

I vividly remember sitting on a United Airlines flight from Chicago to Los Angeles when a friendly looking commercial popped onto a large movie screen in the main cabin of the airplane. An attractive blond woman stood cooking in the kitchen. These words flashed on the screen: "6:00 A.M., prepare breakfast for the family." After a scene change, then came: "7:30 A.M., send the kids to school." After another scene change, "9:30 A.M., clean the house." Finally, "11:00 A.M., *talk to the dead*." The commercial then urged viewers to watch the hit TV series, "*Medium*, 9:00-10:00 P.M. on NBC."

As of this writing, "Medium" still airs weekly amidst rave reviews. The official NBC "Medium" Web site says it's about a special woman who "sees what others can't."[3] "Medium" chronicles the life of Allison DuBois, a vivacious blond lady who helps police solve homicides by using her "gift," *the ability to see and talk to dead people*. Under "Bios," the NBC web site lists Patricia Arquette as the lead actress who plays DuBois, but below Patricia's name, the real "Allison DuBois" is listed as "Consultant/Real-life Medium."

Allison DuBois is a real person behind the show. DuBois' *New York Times* best-selling book, *Don't Kiss Them Goodbye*, recounts her life story, offers factual details about her experiences assisting law enforcement, and explains how she first became involved with departed spirits in the first place. The book's back cover reports:

> When she was six years old, Allison's deceased great-grandfather came to her with a message for her mother: "I am okay, I am still with you. Tell your mom there's no more pain." Allison shared his comforting message with her mother and thus began a lifetime of creating connections between loved ones and those they have lost."[4]

Thus the Hollywood TV series "Medium" is based on the real-life experiences of the real Allison DuBois, who communicates with real spirits.

The CBS network competes with NBC. Recognizing the incredible interest in beyond-the-veil visitations, CBS has created a highly popular parallel series, "Ghost Whisperer", to rival "Medium". The CBS Web site for Ghost Whisperer gives this description of its storyline:

> Ever since she was a young girl, Melinda Gordon (Jennifer Love Hewitt) has been able to see and talk to dead people—earthbound spirits who have yet to cross over to the Other Side and who seek her help in communicating and resolving unfinished business with the living...Although Melinda embraces her unique "abilities" as a blessing and sometimes a curse, she always helps her clients—alive or dead—find emotional closure. [5]

Does "Ghost Whisperer" have any connection with our real world, like "Medium" does? Indeed. Directly below "Show" and "About" on the CBS site, the name "James Van Praagh" is listed. Van Praagh is "Ghost Whisperer's" Co-Executive Producer. The CBS Web site declares:

> James Van Praagh is recognized as one of the foremost mediums in the world. His unique paranormal experiences during the past 22 years have been recorded in his best-selling books: *Talking to Heaven, Reaching to Heaven, Healing Grief—Reclaiming Life After Any Loss, and Heaven and Earth—Making the Psychic Connection*. He has introduced his practices to teenagers with the book *Looking Beyond: A Teens' Guide to the Spiritual World*. His book, *Meditations With James Van Praagh*, brought a new awareness to the mediation experience.
>
> Van Praagh's television credits include producing "Living With the Dead," inspired by his first book, *Talking to Heaven*, and "The Dead Will Tell" for CBS, as well as his own syndicated daytime talk show, "Beyond With James Van Praagh." He has appeared on several television shows including "48 HOURS", "Oprah", and "Larry King Live". [6]

Thus once again, just as real-life medium Allison DuBois is the lead consultant and inspiration behind NBC's "Medium", even so has best-selling author, TV personality, and real-life medium, James Van Praagh, become the Co-Executive Producer and inspiration behind CBS's "Ghost Whisperer". Both Van Praagh and DuBois claim to have inside tracks with the dead. As far as television goes, these two shows are just the tip of the proverbial iceberg.

Some time ago my wife Kristin and I were vacationing in scenic Monterey, California, at the time of our yearly wedding anniversary. Halfway through a relaxing evening together, I decided to surf the listings on our hotel TV for any "family-friendly" programs. *White Noise* appeared as one option, beside a photo of a man and his son. No description or preview was available. Thinking it might be a kosher film about a dad and his boy, I clicked "Watch Now." Minutes later, I clicked the "Power Off" button. Shortly thereafter I walked into Wal-Mart and saw a large rack filled with *White Noise* DVDs. I didn't buy one.

White Noise is a scary movie about a man and his son who endure unspeakable grief after "Mom" fails to come home one night. To their horror and dismay, the mother is killed in a freak car accident where her head is gashed and her body slides into a river. (The "father/son" preview image on the TV set was a scene from the funeral service.) A few days later, the heart-broken husband hears his cell phone ring. Glancing at Caller ID, he is startled as a familiar name appears on the tiny screen. *The caller was his wife.* As this thriller advances, the husband discovers that his deceased spouse is trying to communicate with him through the "white noise" (or static) of common electronic devices. In the movie, this mysterious communication process is given a distinct name, Electronic Voice Phenomenon, otherwise known as EVP.

Is *White Noise* just another fictitious Hollywood movie, or are there similar real-life connections as with "Medium" and "Ghost Whisperer"? A simple Internet search for "Electronic Voice Phenomenon" or EVP will reveal the answer. EVP is real, and it's easy to research its history, theory, and current proponents. There's even an American Association of Electronic Voice

Phenomenon dedicated to capturing actual recordings from invisible entities that have supposedly survived their last earthly breath.[7]

There's an official White Noise movie Web site.[8] Believe me, it's spooky, very spooky. The home page says, *"White Noise: The Line Separating the Living From the Dead Has Been Crossed."* Once inside this Web site, a few clicks lead a person to this bold announcement: *"The following recordings are real."* A few more clicks allow the Internet surfer to hear and watch actual "transmissions" originating from real ghosts (I don't recommend hearing or watching any of these recordings). The *White Noise* movie Web site also offers this overview:

> Electronic Voice Phenomenon—EVP—is the process by which the dead, through sound and image, communicate with the living through the static and white noise of electronic recording devices.
>
> By modest estimates, there are nearly seven billion audio and video recording devices in homes around the world and every one of them is a portal.
>
> For two decades now, a quiet worldwide movement has gained momentum among the growing number of people who believe in EVP and who themselves have captured extraordinary recordings of communications from the dead. These transmissions, recorded from simple household electronic devices, force us to question our basic notions about life and death and seem to confirm what many of us have dared to believe: it is possible for the dead to communicate with us.[9]

Thus NBC's "Medium", CBS's "Ghost Whisperer", and the Hollywood thriller *White Noise* all have connections with the mystical world of non-fiction spirit communication. EVP is a "worldwide movement" gaining "momentum," declare its advocates, and the *White Noise* movie, its official

Web site, and even the *White Noise* DVD itself—which contains a "chilling guide" filled with do-it-yourself instruction about how to contact a dead person—are all part of this worldwide movement. Therefore if ten-year-old Johnny can convince his mom, dad, auntie, grandma, or grandpa to purchase a *White Noise* DVD at Wal-Mart, he'll not only have one extremely scary movie to watch, but lots of information about how to capture actual messages from his deceased relatives in his own bedroom by using an audiotape recorder, VCR, or other recording device. Parents, if this bothers you, keep a close eye on what your kids buy!

Again, "Medium", "Ghost Whisperer", and *White Noise* are just the tip of the iceberg. Because this type of programming nets incredibly positive cash flow for studios, theaters, and networks, Hollywood has become obsessed with churning out films and television series sporting talking-to-the-dead story lines or scenes. *The Sixth Sense* (1999) was a huge success, revolving around "A boy who communicates with spirits that don't know they're dead."[10] *Living With the Dead* (2002) still advertises, "The dead are talking. One man is listening."[11] *Talking Dead* (2005) featured "Doctor Clark" who "invented a machine that allows communication from the dead."[12] NBC's six-part apocalyptic thriller *Revelations* (2005) swirled around messages predicting "the end of days" whispered by the spirit of a dead teenager through the lips of a comatose child.[13] Even the wildly popular *Harry Potter* movies often show Harry in the Hogwarts School of Witchcraft and Wizardry bathroom having conversations with Moaning Myrtle, the ghost of a dead student.[14] There's no doubt that Hollywood is currently mesmerized by the spirit world. So are theater and DVD viewers.

In addition to DuBois and Van Praagh, there are myriads of TV personalities claiming beyond-the-veil connections. One of the best known is psychic expert, best-selling author, and globetrotting lecturer John Edward who dazzles audiences worldwide with his "unique abilities to connect people with loved ones who have passed on."[15] His popular TV show, "Crossing Over

With John Edward" (1999-2004), linked the living with the dead through "readings" in which Mr. Edward received "thought messages" from dead relatives of those in his audience.

Carla Mae, host of her TV show "Messages", is yet another who "connects to people's deceased loved ones."[16] As does Sylvia Browne. In her *New York Times* best-selling *Life on the Other Side*, Browne explains how "spirits came into her room at night" when she was a child and then reports on her many subsequent "conversations with a spirit guide named Francine."[17] Browne is a regular guest on *The Montel Williams Show* and has appeared on "Larry King Live", "Good Morning America", "CNN", and "Entertainment Tonight".

On October 30, 2006, "The Lisa Williams Project" hit the airwaves. The series revolves around British medium Lisa Williams who communicates "with friends and family who have passed into the Spirit World."[18] The 29-year-old Williams is a now a rising star. As I write this, William's Web site says, "Lisa is currently in the USA...filming her new show for Lifetime TV." Produced by Merv Griffin Entertainment, "The Lisa Williams Project" airs on the Lifetime television network, a leader in women's entertainment, owned by Lifetime Entertainment Services, "a 50/50 joint venture of The Hearst Corporation and The Walt Disney Company."[19]

What sets "The Lisa Williams Project" apart from "Medium", "Ghost Whisperer", and other Hollywood movies is that it is entirely non-fiction, with no actors and actresses. In other words, it's a "reality show"—the real thing. A Griffin Group Press Release explains:

> Shot around southern California, each episode of "The Lisa Williams Project" (wt) follows Lisa interacting with ordinary Americans as they go about their daily lives—in their homes, at work and play, in the supermarket or on the street.
>
> In these impromptu meetings, Lisa relays messages from the dead to their astonished relatives and friends. Amid laughter and tears, she

passes along words of love or forgiveness, solves a misunderstanding, helps someone to say good-bye, or explains something as mundane as the whereabouts of misplaced keys. The series also observes Lisa afterwards, for a glimpse of how these stories affect her personal life with her husband, Kevin, and her six-year-old son, Charlie, who already shows an inherited gift for natural healing and talking with spirits.[20]

By the time you read this, new TV shows will probably have started. Now you know why that unnamed author in *People* magazine wondered, "What is it with the dearly departed? Seems they're everywhere lately. Ghosts, ghouls and spirits are invading prime time ["Medium", "Ghost Whisperer", "Supernatural"] and buying secondhand yachts for pop psychics like John Edward."[21]

Spirits invading prime time?

What on earth (or in the atmosphere) is going on? Is this all just Hollywood hype, or is something truly supernatural occurring behind the scenes? *Are real bodiless intelligences communicating information to famous mediums and TV personalities?* If so, can we trust their insights? How do mediums like Allison DuBois, James Van Praagh, John Edward, Carla Mae, Sylvia Browne, Lisa Williams, and countless others who are now holding intimate "conversations" with invisible entities know for sure that their otherworldly guides are truly friendly?

Is it possible that these invisible informants are really tricksters with sinister motives?

You will find out soon.

ENDNOTES

1.   Allison DuBois, *Don't Kiss Them Goodbye* (New York: Simon and Shuster, 2004).

2.   "They See Dead People," *People* (November 7, 2005).

3.   See http://www.nbc.com/Medium/.

4.   DuBois, *Don't Kiss Them Goodbye*, back cover.

5.   See http://www.cbs.com/primetime/ghost_whisperer/about/.

6.   See http://www.cbs.com/primetime/ghost_whisperer/bios/praagh.shtml.

7.   See http://aaevp.com/.

8.   See http://www.whitenoisemovie.com/.

9.   See http://www.whitenoisemovie.com/.

10. See http://us.imdb.com/title/tt0167404/.

11. See http://www.imdb.com/title/tt0289652/.

12. See http://www.imdb.com/title/tt0844027/maindetails.

13. See http://www.tv.com/revelations/hour-one/episode/421092/summary.html.

14. J.K. Rowling, *Harry Potter and the Chamber of Secrets* (New York: Scholastic Publications, 1999), 156.

15. Taken from the official John Edward Web site. See http://johnedward.net/about_John_Edward.htm.

16. Taken from the official Carla Mae Web site. See http://carlamae.com/.

17. An "Editorial Review" by Amazon.com of *Life on the Other Side*, by Sylvia Browne (2002). Posted on Amazon.com.

18. Taken from Lisa William's Web site. See http://www.lisawilliams.uk.com/.

19. Taken from The Merv Griffin Entertainment Web site. See http://www.merv.com/index.cfm/fuseaction/category.display/category_id/107/index.cfm.

20. Taken from The Merv Griffin Entertainment Web site. See http://www.merv.com/index.cfm/fuseaction/category.display/category_id/107/index.cfm.

21. See endnote 2.

Chapter 2

VOICES FROM BEYOND

Ghosts cross every culture and continent, and the belief in their existence is on the rise.

—Our Haunted Lives: True Life Ghost Encounters[1]

S CIENCE has its limits, and life is permeated with the unexplainable. Skeptics may scoff, yet history is full of people who have relayed convincing personal stories of meeting beyond-this-world visitors. In our 21st century, the number of these stories is increasing rapidly. You are about to read just a few of these unusual encounters. The first three were reported in that "They See Dead People" article in *People* magazine referred to previously. Face-to-face meetings with phantoms caused some to merely chuckle. Others were scared out of their wits.

FRANKLIN, TENN. Come Christmastime, Tom Murdic gets a jolly visitor in his home. Not Santa, but an apparition that looks like a young black boy in a Civil War-era puffy shirt. The ghost turns on appliances and bangs on walls but is otherwise, says Murdic, a good kid. "He's more of a curiosity," than a terror. Murdic, 51, a county planning commissioner, explains, "But then I don't scare easily."

His wife and kids do, though, and they're not crazy about the ghost that has turned up especially during winters every year since the Murdics bought their home—on land that was once a Confederate army encampment—in 1993. Tom's daughter Cathy, 24, has felt him tap her on the head, and his wife, Deborah, heard voices in the garage but walked in to find only her agitated dog barking at no one. His son Nick, 30, was home alone when he heard a loud pounding on a wall. "It freaked me out," he says, "and I left." Tom's the only one to get a good look: He saw the boy walk across the kitchen and disappear into the dishwasher. As long as he doesn't run up the electric bill, says Murdic, the little guy can stay. "He's just one of those anomalies," he says, "that we just don't quite understand."[2]

Who is this "little guy" who shows up each year around Christmastime and mysteriously switches on microwave ovens and bangs on walls? Is he really the ghost of "a young black boy" from Civil War days? You will discover the answer soon.

OXFORD, MICH. You're 6 years old and lying in bed when a woman's face—no body, just a face—materializes in your room. Um, who you gonna call? "It was just weird," remembers Kirsten Jorgensen, 22, who says a ghost appeared to her in full body form on and off for 10 years in the 155-year-old house where she lived with her brother and parents. Another time "I saw her walking with a bird on her shoulder," says Jorgensen. "I fainted."

But then she grew fond of the ghost—and credits it with saving her life. One night when Jorgensen was 16, the ghost—whom she believes was Carrie Crawford, a veterinarian's wife who died in Kirsten's bedroom in the 1930's—woke her up and led her to the hall.

There, claims Jorgenson, she saw smoke coming from under her brother Ian's bedroom door—a candle had started a fire. "I ran downstairs and got the fire extinguisher and put it out," says Jorgensen, who never saw the ghost again. Today Jorgensen—an anthropology major at Oakland University—accepts her experience as just another part of a unique childhood. "Growing up, I was that creepy girl who lived in the haunted house," she says. "Today my friends think it's cool."[3]

Kirsten's poltergeist seems friendly enough, even life-saving. At first her experience looked "creepy" to her classmates, but no more. Now it's "cool." Considering that *People* magazine "is the most wildly, consistently successful magazine in history,"[4] Jorgensen's reportedly creepy-to-cool transition seems to mirror what's happening within society at large. Having conversations with ghosts has become an "in thing." Hollywood surely thinks so.

ORANGEVALE, CA. When Rhonda Witter first walked through the three-bedroom, 1,400-sq.-ft. ranch house, she liked it enough to want to buy it—even though she felt she was being watched by unseen eyes. When she took her kids, Sarah, 8, and Garrett, 10, to have a look, they liked it too—except, she says, for the specter that materialized. "Sara said, 'You do know there's an old man in the bathroom?'" recalls Witter, 43, who is divorced. "I told her, 'I know, it's okay. He can stay.'"

And so he has. Not long after moving in this February, Witter claims she had her first chat with the ghost. "He smokes cigarettes, so I woke up smelling smoke," she says. "I asked him what his name was, but he didn't answer. Yet there was something protective about him. My kids think of him as a grandfather figure." Since then they've worked out some ground rules—"I told him he needs to smoke outside"—and even found a way for the old guy to earn his keep. "I'd be getting the kids ready for school, and they'd tell me they couldn't find their socks," says Witter. "Then they'd scream, 'Here they are, on the table!' I didn't put them there, and neither did they." That's why Witter has no plans to evict the boarder. "He is old and grumpy," she says, "but he's lovable too, and I like having him here."[5]

A "lovable" grumpy ghost who helps boys and girls find their socks? With such reports as this, it's understandable why more and more people don't mind cozying up with invisible entities. "Most ghosts are totally neutral and mean no harm," says prominent ghost hunter Richard L. Senate, author of *Ghosts of the Haunted Coast: Ghost Hunting on California's Gold Coast.* Senate's perspective is fast becoming the conviction of millions living in the New Millennium.

Countless books have been written containing reports from those who claim to have met the Returning Dead. The list below is but a short sample. These writers are not fly-by-nights but esteemed authors and speakers who have captivated public attention and been interviewed on national TV and radio shows. Their books and conclusions often involve careful, apparently scientific research.

- *We Don't Die: George Anderson's Conversations With the Other Side* by Joel Martin (Berkley Publishing Group, 1989).

- *The Dead Are Alive: They Can & Do Communicate With You* by Harold Sherman (Fawcett Books, 1997).

- *Hello From Heaven: A New Field of Research-After-Death Communication Confirms That Life and Love Are Eternal* by Bill and Judy Guggenheim (Bantam Books, 1997).

- *Messages: Evidence for Life After Death* by George E. Dalzell and Gary E. Schwartz (Hampton Roads Publishing Company, 2002).

- *The Afterlife Experiments: Breakthrough Scientific Evidence of Life After Death* by Gary E. Schwartz and William L. Simon (Atria, 2002).

- *Visits From the Afterlife: The Truth About Hauntings, Spirits, and Reunions With Lost Loved Ones* by Sylvia Browne (New American Library, 2003).

- *Communicating With the Dead: Reach Beyond the Grave* by Jeff Belanger (New Page Books, 2005).

- *The Truth About Medium: Extraordinary Experiments With the Real Allison DuBois of NBC's Medium and other Remarkable Psychics* by Gary E. Schwartz and William L. Simon (Hampton Roads Publishing Co., 2005).

- *How to Talk to the Other Side: Learning How to Communicate With Loved Ones, Spirits and Angels* by Dr. Gary Fearn, D.D. (Trafford Publishing, 2006).

As mentioned before, Sylvia Browne is one of the most popular talk-to-the-dead authors and TV personalities of the 21st century. "We sell lots of her books," said an employee at a B. Dalton's bookstore in Fresno, California as we chatted at the cash register while I purchased Allison DuBois' *Don't Kiss Them Goodbye*, Leslie Rule's *Coast to Coast Ghosts*, and Browne's *Visits From the Afterlife* on my Visa card. As with countless other books, each of these supernaturally permeated productions is filled with stories, accounts, descriptions, sightings, and conversations involving those who have sensed, seen, felt, touched, and spoken to invisible personalities floating about without bodies—all of whom are assumed to be the spirits of dead people.

In the Epilogue of *Visits From the Afterlife*, Sylvia Browne concludes her book with "My Favorite Ghost Story." Because Browne is so popular, because this story provides such a unique window into the life of one of the world's most respected mediums, and because there are elements I wish to comment upon later, I have decided to reproduce it in its entirety. Get ready for one amazing ghost story! Sylvia Browne testifies:

It was 1990, and my life was busier than ever. I was in my twentieth year of television appearances on everything from talk shows to *In Search Of* and more network specials than I can remember. I was touring the country giving lectures, I was averaging about twenty private readings a day, and I was devoting countless pro bono hours to my consultation work with both law enforcement and the medical community. In fact, looking back, I might have been trying to stay too busy to think. I was just recovering from a serious personal crisis, proving once again that I don't have a psychic bone in my body about my own personal life, and I tend to compulsively run myself ragged when I'm fighting my way out of a depression.

So when an invitation came out of nowhere to do a haunting investigation of the Queen Mary in the Long Beach, California harbor, I said yes before I had time to realize that my schedule and I were already on serious overload. I wasn't even quite sure who'd issued the invitation. I caught the name "Herman," and something about a brother and a Halloween show, and a reference to CBS, with whom I'd enjoyed a long-standing relationship. I also noticed that the date they wanted me happened to coincide with a trip to Los Angeles I'd committed to anyway, so I had nothing to lose but a few hours I couldn't really spare. And when you're in the middle of compulsive workaholism, it doesn't get much more irresistible than that.

Stepping onto the Queen Mary, if you've never had the experience, is like stepping into a beautiful, gleaming, elegant past-life dream. There is dark, polished, inlaid mahogany everywhere, with gorgeous brass railings and massive crystal chandeliers, history preserved in exquisite craftsmanship. I was wondering why such stunning surroundings felt so oppressive when a young production intern dashed up, welcomed me, and offered to show me the cabin where I would be spending the night. With apologies, she explained that "Our Host" wouldn't be joining us until the next day, as if I might be terribly disappointed about a delay in meeting someone I'd never heard of. I kept my apathy to myself and simply assured her that I was too preoccupied with the idea of meeting the ghosts on board, if there were any, to worry about when Our Host was arriving.

My cabin was as lovely as the dinner I was served, and throughout the meal I kept my antennae up for any ghosts or spirits who might be hanging around trying to get my attention. Nothing. I smiled to myself, a little perversely, as I pictured a Halloween special in which I walked Our Host around this huge ship for an hour on film saying over and over again, "Nope. Sorry. There's nothing here." But Halloween special or not, if I came to the conclusion that the Queen Mary wasn't haunted, there was no way I would ever claim it was, just for the sake of ratings, or to feel that I gave these people their money's worth. This was their bright idea, after all, not mine.

I hadn't realized until I sank into bed how exhausted I was. In fact, I was almost too exhausted to realize that I'd become a banquet for swarms of mosquitoes that were flying in and out through the open porthole of my cabin. I finally swatted my way to the porthole, slammed it shut, and went back to bed, only to discover after a few minutes that with the porthole closed, the cabin was sweltering hot and the still air was so stifling I could barely breath. Great choice, I thought, feeling sorrier for myself by the minute. Being eaten alive by mosquitoes, or smothering to death. I finally opted for the mosquitoes and stomped over to open the porthole again.

It was at that moment, well past midnight, that I heard footprints running up and down the hall outside my door. I didn't think much about it at first. There was a whole television production team and crew on board, so it could easily have been any one of them. But the more I listened the more I realized that these sounded like awfully tiny feet, taking awfully tiny steps, to belong to any of the production staff. I crept to the door and very quietly opened it. And there in the hallway, playfully dashing around all over the place, was the very real but indistinct ghost of a little boy. He was filmy, more like a figure made of white smoke than anything solid, but I could make out knickers and a newsboy cap on his small frame. He didn't talk to me, didn't even notice me, just kept right on playing what looked like a solitary game of tag, and after watching him for several minutes I left him to his private illusions and fell into bed among the mosquitoes again, thinking as I drifted off to sleep that maybe this Halloween special wouldn't be completely uneventful after all.

I was sleepy, cranky, and very itchy the next morning when I told the production team about the little ghost boy in the hallway, and you've never seen a less impressed group of people in your life. I had no details to offer, since the boy never spoke to me and I couldn't get a clear enough image of him to come up with any psychic facts I could rely on, and there were certainly no witnesses, so the reactions ranged from polite patronizing to blatant eye-rolling. The crew was wondering what kind of lunatic they were stuck with and I was wondering if any of them cared how miserably tired and mosquito-bitten I was when the young intern I'd met the day before flew by to suggest we start the tour without Our Host.

"He'll catch up with you shortly," she excitedly assured me.

Who cares? I muttered silently to myself.

We followed orders and started our tour of this gorgeous ship— or, as I was now thinking of it thanks to my mood, this stupid boat. Audiotapes were rolling and cameras were at the ready to capture my every encounter with every ghost and spirit we ran into along the way. The problem was, there weren't any. Cabin after cabin, deck after deck, from the dining rooms to the ballroom to the magnificent captain's quarters, there wasn't even a hint of the afterlife to be found. Not even the little ghost boy from the night before put in an appearance. My fear of being part of the dullest Halloween special in history, kind of Sylvia Browne version of Geraldo Rivera unearthing Al Capone's vault, was becoming more and more real by the minute.

After what seemed like weeks, we reached the lowest deck on the ship, where it looked as if a swimming pool used to be. And suddenly, to my complete surprise, a ghost, as real and distinct and in full color as the rest of us, materialized out of nowhere. I stopped cold, then stepped forward. The crew stayed where they were, not seeing a thing but rolling their cameras on the off chance I wasn't crazy.

She was young, maybe nineteen or twenty. She was wearing a midcalf-length white party dress, a sleeveless sheath with heavy beading at the hem, a long strand of pearls around her neck, very much like a flapper from the 1920s would wear. She had on opaque white stockings and white low-heeled Mary Jane shoes. Her hair was short and jet black, in finger waves framing her face. Her eyes were dark, dramatic, and slightly Indian looking, reminiscent of Merle Oberon, the strikingly lovely actress whom I've probably watched fifty times in the classic Wuthering Heights with Laurence Olivier. She was dancing, arms high in the air, and when I stepped toward her she changed course and began twirling in circles around and around me. There was no joy in her wild, whirling dance. Instead, it looked frantic and driven, and the incessant smile on her face seemed much more insane than happy. All ghosts are desperately confused and disoriented, of course, but I'd never seen one as manic as this one.

I asked her what her name was.

"Mary," she said, spinning closer, pleased to be noticed and acknowledged. She looked up and down at me and added, "You're dressed so oddly."

Any impulse I might have had to offer up the pot-calling-the-kettle-black cliché was lost immediately when, for the first time, I could see angry red open wounds on the inside of both her wrists. It didn't take a psychic to figure out that she had taken her own life, and I asked her if the cuts hurt her.

"Not anymore," she laughed, and then added defensively, "and they're not cuts. They're just scratches."

"No, they're deep cuts, Mary," I said quietly. "Tell me what happened."

She never stopped moving, never stopped her dizzying dance as she told me her story, her occasional giggling inappropriate for such a tragic chain of events. There was a man. His name was Robert. She was deeply in love with him and had accepted his proposal of marriage. Then, with no warning and no apologies, he simply vanished one day, running off to marry another woman he'd decided might be more to his financial advantage, she later found out. Mary was disconsolate, and her parents, whom she called "Mommy" and "Daddy" in what sounded like a contrived childlike voice, virtually dragged her onto the Queen Mary as the first leg of a three-month trip to Europe they hoped would mend her broken heart and help her forget about this man they'd never approved of in the first place. As far as Mary was concerned, this was the third day of their cruise—in other words, very probably the day she'd descended to the lowest deck of the ship and killed herself.

"You know what's going to happen?" she laughed, dropping her voice to a low, secretive manner as she twirled by.

"What's going to happen?"

"He's going to leave her and come back to me. You'll see, he's going to wire me through the ship's captain and tell me he's waiting for me in England."

I wanted to tell her that Robert was dead. I wanted to tell her that *she* was dead, so that she could go Home and finally be at peace. I approached the subject gently, knowing how seriously disturbed she was. "Mary," I started, "you can be with Robert right now if you'll let me help..."

I was interrupted by a quiet baritone voice behind me, asking, "Who in the world are you talking to?"

I turned around and found myself looking into the beautiful, sensitive face of a man who was so obviously charismatic I knew he had to be our long-awaited Host. My dear friend and co-writer Lindsey describes rare moments like that one, in which you meet a stranger who seems inexplicably familiar the instant your eyes meet, as a feeling of wanting to say, "Oh, *there* you are. I've never heard of you, but I've been waiting for you to come into my life." I actually blushed, partly because I realized that, from his point of view he'd just caught me having a rather emotional conversation with myself, and partly because his eye contact was so intense.

We introduced ourselves, and then I quickly began telling him about Mary and her tragic story, not sure if I was making myself less crazy or more as I explained that no, I wasn't chatting with myself, I was chatting with a ghost. She was twirling wildly around both of us now, and I noticed that she was listening intently and vain enough to love knowing that we were talking about her. Our Host listened intently, without judgment, the exact kind of open-minded skeptic I appreciate.

"She's here right now?" he asked.

I nodded.

"What's she doing?"

"She's whirling around us in a circle, like she's been doing since I got here," I told him. For some reason at that moment it occurred to me that she was in a sleeveless dress in the chilly air of the bottom deck, and I turned to her and said, "Aren't you cold?"

"Why do you think I'm dancing?" she answered. Her tone reminded me exactly of my granddaughter Angelia's tone when she thinks I've asked a stupid question. I decided Mary was probably a Scorpio too.

Our Host, in the meantime, was looking all around, clearly unable to see Mary but genuinely wanting to if, in fact, she existed. There was no way I could help make that happen, but if he was open to the idea of experiencing her, there was one thing I knew might be worth trying.

First, I told Mary to stand still. She loved all this attention so much that she actually did it. Then I took Our Host by the hand. He was brave enough not to hesitate, even though he didn't have a clue what I was about to do. And then, without a word, I simply walked him right through Mary's ghostly body.

I'll never forget how huge his eyes were after he'd stepped through her. "Oh, my God!" was all he said, clearly shaken.

"Did you feel that?" It was a rhetorical question. I could look at him and tell he felt it.

"Feel it? How could I *not* feel it?" he replied. "Whatever it was, it was freezing cold."

I decided to play the devil's advocate. "Well, to be fair, it is chilly down here."

He shook his head. "Not like that. That wasn't any kind of cold I've ever felt. It went all the way through me, right down to my bones, and just in that one spot you walked me through."

"Anything else?" I asked.

"Absolutely," he said, shuddering a little. "It was like walking through a wall of cobwebs. I can still feel them all over me."

I'd had that same feeling myself during ghost encounters, and I knew that even though the sensation itself would pass quickly, he would never forget it. I smiled and kept my response to a simple "So now you've met Mary."

He just nodded and looked at me. All the skepticism was gone from his eyes. He believed. I didn't convince him. Mary did.

Mary had lost all interest in us by now and went whirling away into her own lost world again. The producer and several members of the crew were excited to tell me that it was on this lowest deck, in this exact spot, where the employees of the Queen Mary had heard the most unexplainable noises, seen the most unexplainable visions of something filmy white, and been the most frightened. I wasn't surprised. I appreciated the validation.

Our Host suggested we go find a place to sit. I'm sure he needed a chance to regroup, and I was grateful for a chance to quietly and privately learn more about this handsome, charismatic, oddly familiar stranger. We settled onto a bench on an upper deck and started talking.

To this day, all these years later, we haven't stopped.

As most of you probably figured out pages and pages ago, our host's name was Montel Williams.

That's how we met.

And that's why the Queen Mary is and always will be my favorite ghost story.[7]

So now you know how TV host Montel Williams became a believer in ghosts. To this day, Sylvia Browne is still a regular guest on his show. In the last few years, the number of believers—like Montel Williams—has multiplied exponentially, as has the number of mediums like Sylvia Browne whose work and psychic insights are increasingly recognized by the public as legitimate.

Again, all of the authors whose books I have listed in this chapter believe the ghosts they are encountering are the spirits of deceased humans. As a result of their research, experiments, personal encounters, or conversations with witnesses, these authors are attempting to prove that the dead really aren't dead, that they've merely passed over to another dimension, that communication with these entities is possible, that we can learn important truths from them, and that their existence offers immeasurable comfort that this life "isn't all there is."

I don't doubt the sincerity of these authors, or question their motives. Neither do I seek to pass judgment on their personal lives or eternal destinies. On the surface, their research does indeed sound comforting. But as you shall soon discover, there's immeasurably more to this wildly popular talking-to-the-dead phenomenon than what is observable by naked eyes, or even psychic eyes.

When Montel Williams stepped through Mary's ghost, he declared, "That wasn't any kind of cold I've ever felt. It went all the way through me, right down to my bones." In *Don't Kiss Them Goodbye*, Allison DuBois candidly confessed, "When I am preparing for a private reading, I know the

Other Side is churning around me when my hands quickly become freezing. I refer to this as holding hands with the Other Side."[8]

I hate to say it, but the *real truth* is colder and more chilling than either Montel Williams or Allison DuBois realize.

Get ready for it.

ENDNOTES

1. Publisher comment about *Our Haunted Lives* by Jeff Belanger. See http://search.barnesandnoble.com/booksearch/isbninquiry.asp?ean= 9781564148568&z=y#PUB.

2. "They See Dead People," *People* (November 7, 2005).

3. "They See Dead People," *People* (November 7, 2005).

4. Product Description of *People* magazine from Amazon.com. See http://www.amazon.com/People-6-Month-Subscription-5-Bonus/dp/B00005R8BC.

5. "They See Dead People," *People* (November 7, 2005).

6. Quoted in *People*.

7. Sylvia Browne (with Lindsey Harrison), *Visits From the Afterlife: The Truth About Hauntings, Spirits, and Reunions With Lost Loved Ones* (London: New American Library, a division of Penguin books, 2003), 261-268.

8. Allison DuBois, *Don't Kiss Them Goodbye* (New York: Simon and Shuster, 2004), 102-103.

Chapter 3

AFTERLIFE
EXPERIMENTS

Appearances often are deceiving.

—Aesop (620 B.C.-520 B.C.), *The Wolf in Sheep's Clothing*

A RE modern mediums receiving *real messages* from the Other Side, or is it all just a trick? For over a decade Dr. Gary E. Schwartz, Ph.D., has been determined to find out. Professor of psychology, medicine, neurology, psychiatry, and surgery at the University of Arizona in Tucson and director of its Human Energy Systems Laboratory, Dr. Schwartz has conducted scientific experiments on professional mediums to test their "skills." Schwartz isn't a crackpot, but a man with credible academic achievements under his belt. After receiving his doctorate from Harvard University, he served as a professor of psychology and psychiatry at Yale University, director of the Yale Psychophysiology Center, and co-director of the Yale Behavioral Medicine Clinic. He has published more than 400 scientific papers, edited 11 academic books, and co-authored numerous hot-selling books. His most popular books include:

- *The Living Energy Universe* by Gary E. Schwartz and Linda G.S. Russek (Hampton Roads Publishing Company, 1999).

- *The Afterlife Codes: Searching for Evidence of the Survival of the Soul* by Susy Smith, Gary E.R. Schwartz, and Linda G.S. Russek (Hampton Roads Publishing Company, 2000).

- *The Afterlife Experiments: Breakthrough Scientific Evidence of Life After Death* by Deepak Chopra, Gary E. Schwartz, and William Simon (Atria, 2003).

- *The Truth About Medium: Extraordinary Experiments With the Real Allison DuBois of NBC's Medium and other Remarkable Psychics* by Gary E. Schwartz and William L. Simon (Hampton Roads Publishing Company, 2005).

Beginning in the 1990s, Dr. Gary Schwartz has conducted "afterlife experiments" on famous mediums, such as John Edward, Suzanne Northrop, George Anderson, Anne Gehman, and Laurie Campbell. From 2001–2004, Allison DuBois became one of the "test cases." It all started when DuBois was watching NBC's "Dateline" and saw a story about Dr. Schwartz's experiments with John Edward. In her book, *Don't Kiss Them Goodbye*, DuBois revealed:

> My guides told me that I was to be part of Dr. Schwartz's research and that I had to contact him. My guides never steer me wrong, but I knew nothing about being a research medium...It took about a month to get in to meet with this busy man. If you're a psychic looking for confirmation from Gary that you're significant, forget it. Gary looks at you to study you, not to praise you. I like that about him. He's a scientist, not a groupie. I now sarcastically refer to myself as Gary's lab rat.[1]

After making initial contact with Dr. Schwartz, about a month later Allison went to Tucson, Arizona, to meet the professor at the University. After some friendly chitchat, Schwartz revealed that the timing of this appointment was significant, for he had just lost someone special only two days before. "While Gary was talking," DuBois reflects, "I saw a male spirit standing next to him."[2] After informing Schwartz of this, he responded coolly, "Yes, that's fine. We'll talk about that after I test you." What interested Dr. Schwartz at that moment was not the male ghost DuBois claimed to "see," but what messages or details she might get about his deceased friend—a woman—whom he had just referred to. About this special person, Schwartz "provided no other information—not age, gender, or circumstance."[3]

Allison became really nervous. Relying totally on "her guides," she was hoping this meeting wouldn't end in embarrassment. They didn't disappoint her. After a short pause, Allison declared, "I see an old woman. She's petite with white hair and she has a small dog with her." Schwartz sat silently for a moment. "Go on," he said. Then Allison was "flashed a picture" and continued, "I see a paperboy selling newspapers on a street corner; he's in New York City. He's holding up the newspaper and showing it to me. The person on the Other Side is saying, 'I do not walk alone.'"[4]

Schwartz took notes without comment. Allison then relayed other details that "came to her." When the session was over, Dr. Schwartz said, "Let me tell you what the information means." Here is DuBois' account of what the doctor said:

> He started off by telling me that the person who had just died was named Susy Smith and was in fact an old woman. She was eighty-nine, just shy of her ninetieth birthday. They had been colleagues and good friends. She was petite and had white hair, and had once been a newspaper reporter in New York City. And, indeed, she had a little dog she had loved that had died years ago.

The statement "I do not walk alone" was also significant to Gary. Susy had stated before she died that she hoped she'd be able to walk again on the Other Side. She had relied heavily on a wheelchair at the time of her death. Susy was letting Gary know that she was whole again. Also, she loved children but had none of her own. I had described her as standing beside a male child. Susy is now taking care of children; she was mothering them. She was letting Gary know that she walks among children on the Other Side...There were many other details that let Gary know that she was alive and well on the Other Side.[5]

Then they discussed the "male spirit" Allison saw earlier, and other details Schwartz confirmed to be true. As with many previous experiments the professor had conducted at the University of Arizona, once again, right in front of him, was compelling evidence of an individual who genuinely had the "gift"—an ability to see dead people. After passing her first test, Allison breathed a sigh of relief and reflected, "Confirmation is sweet to a medium."[6]

From 2001–2004, Dr. Schwartz continued testing Allison DuBois. Another situation worth noting occurred in April 2001. DuBois reports:

Dr. Schwartz had [privately] asked a question of his late friend Susy. He wanted Susy to hear his question and send his answer through any of the mediums participating in his study. We were not allowed to know what the question was and we were all tested independently.

Dr. Schwartz asked me if I knew the answer. (There's some pressure!) I kept getting that it was something Susy wanted to bequeath to Dr. Schwartz. I repeatedly saw a scene from *The Wizard of Oz* where Dorothy is holding her little dog, Toto, in a hand basket. I described this and Dr. Schwartz asked me to elaborate on what I was seeing.

While Dr. Schwartz was talking to our secretary-recorder about the notes he was taking, I whispered, "Her dog."

His ears perked right up. "What did you say?"

I said, "Her dog. Who has her dog? She wants you to have her dog; she says no one will love her dog like you will."

I continued, and at the end of our session I was told that the question that Dr. Schwartz had asked Susy was, "Who do you want to take your dog?" That's what I refer to as a psychic high-five score![7]

In January 2005, the *Arizona Daily Star* published reporter Carla McClain's story about Schwartz's experiments with DuBois:

The real-life Phoenix woman who inspired the new TV drama "Medium" can indeed contact dead people, according to scientific—and controversial—tests performed on her at the University of Arizona.

The abilities of Allison Dubois—who claims she can see dead people, receive information from them, and even hear the thoughts of the living—are showcased in the new NBC Monday night show, with actress Patricia Arquette.

In real life, Dubois, 33 next week, has used her paranormal talents to help police in Phoenix and in other states solve crimes—the main plot of "Medium," along with her life as a wife and mother of three young children.

But what few may realize is Dubois' prime power—making contact with people after death—has been subjected to three years of UA research scientifically designed to determine if she is an authentic "medium" or a fraud.

Although the studies have stirred controversy nationwide and have been slammed by several skeptics, the Harvard-trained UA professor who ran them strongly defends their legitimacy, as does Dubois.

"There is no question this is not a fraud—some people really can do this, and Allison is one of them," said psychology professor Gary E. Schwartz, who directs the UA's Human Energy Systems Laboratory where the experiments with Dubois and other well-known mediums—including John Edward of TV's "Crossing Over" fame—have been conducted.

"Many people claim to do this, and there are clearly frauds out there. Allison was repeatedly tested and passed every test.

"As a scientist, I approach all this as an agnostic—I don't believe it; I don't disbelieve it. After testing her under conditions that ruled out the possibility of fraud, I came to the conclusion she's the real deal."[8]

As *The Star* story acknowledged, Dr. Gary Schwartz has his critics—one argument being that DuBois and other "research mediums" aren't 100% accurate. Schwartz responded by saying, "This is like a skeptical sports reviewer focusing on Michael Jordan's few air balls and fouls, and drawing the conclusion that Jordan can't play basketball."[9] Schwartz's point is valid. Even without 100% accuracy (DuBois typically scores in the 70-80% range), discovering specific details that *cannot naturally be known* implies supernatural assistance. Dr. Schwartz's book, *The Afterlife Experiments: Breakthrough Scientific Evidence of Life After Death*, documents case after case, detail after detail, of uncanny revelations to "research mediums" about the personal lives of "sitters" and their deceased loved ones that cannot be explained as originating from normal causes. All of this has convinced Professor Schwartz—and countless others—to abandon skepticism and become a believer.

The Star story concludes with this:

> Just how Allison Dubois could have faked what she told Phran Ginsberg about her teenage daughter Bailey—who died in a car crash two years ago—baffles Ginsberg.
>
> "We were in separate states; we never met. I had no idea who was doing the reading. This was done by phone, and I was not allowed to speak," said Ginsberg, who lives in Lloyd Harbor, N.Y.
>
> The first thing Dubois said was that she saw a photo of her daughter hugging her sister at a party. At that moment, Ginsberg was looking at a photo of the scene.
>
> "Then she told me Bailey wished me 'Happy Valentine's Day.' And that didn't make sense, because it was October," she said. But later that day, she took the photo from its frame, and on the back Bailey had written "Valentine's Day Dance."
>
> "Right then, I knew Allison was the real deal," Ginsberg said. Dubois also had described the accident and Bailey's fatal head injury.
>
> "How could she know this? I just can't see any way she could fake that—she didn't know my name. She didn't know Bailey's name. I see absolutely no other way. This has to be real."[10]

I believe that *it is real.* Indeed, something supernatural is going on. Real mediums do "see" things, receive "messages," and gather "information" from the Other Side that cannot naturally be known.

Who is giving these messages?

DuBois answers, "my guides."

Who are these guides? Be patient. You'll know soon.

Endnotes

1. Allison DuBois, *Don't Kiss Them Goodbye* (New York: Simon and Shuster, 2004), 176-177.

2. DuBois, *Don't Kiss Them Goodbye*, 178.

3. DuBois, *Don't Kiss Them Goodbye*, 178.

4. DuBois, *Don't Kiss Them Goodbye*, 179.

5. DuBois, *Don't Kiss Them Goodbye*, 180.

6. DuBois, *Don't Kiss Them Goodbye*, 181.

7. DuBois, *Don't Kiss Them Goodbye*, 181-182.

8. Carla McClain, "Varied Readings on Arizona Psychic," *Arizona Daily Star* (January 17, 2005). See http://www.azstarnet.com/sn/printDS/57187.

9. McClain, "Varied Readings."

10. McClain, "Varied Readings."

Chapter 4

THE SINISTER SIDE OF SETH

You may call me whatever you choose. I call myself Seth. It fits the me of me.

—Seth, invisible author of eight books[1]

IT all started on the night of December 8, 1963, when American author Jane Roberts (1929-1984) and her husband Robert Butts were experimenting in their Elmira, New York, apartment with a Ouija board as part of Butts' research for a book on Extra-Sensory Perception, or ESP. Unexpectedly, the board's pointer began moving from letter to letter, forming words, then sentences. Robert then asked the board to identify the name of its mysterious operator. "*Seth*," the Ouija board replied. Communication continued, and soon Seth's ideas were flying into Jane's astonished mind faster than they could be written on the board. As Jane later described it, she soon felt like she was perched on top of a high diving board, with others standing behind her impatiently urging her to jump. Finally, Jane made her choice, surrendered herself completely, and took the plunge. Seth took control. Entering a trance-like state, the ghost then began speaking through Jane Roberts, instead of through the Ouija board.

From the outset, "Seth" manifested itself as a distinct, witty, gregarious personality. As Jane yielded to this alien influence, her voice changed, becoming stronger, deeper, and more masculine. "[Jane] acknowledged a sense of great power in Seth's voice."[2] It soon became obvious to Jane, Butts, and many other witnesses of these remarkable events inside that Elmira apartment—including students, journalists, and scientists—that the entity speaking through Jane Roberts' lips *was not Jane Roberts*, but Seth. "The being acted like a jocular, wise, paternal old friend from some past life. Yet it made no mistake in showing that it was fully superhuman and, among other things, [was] trying to get across to this world the wisdom that it was only now ready for."[3] Seth claimed to have existed before planet Earth was formed.

In the months and years that followed, Robert Butts took detailed notes of all public and private "Seth sessions." His early notes were soon published under the title, *How to Develop Your ESP Power* (1966), but this was later changed to *The Coming of Seth*. One day, to Jane and her husband's surprise, Seth announced that he wanted to write his own book. So four nights a week, Jane yielded, Seth talked, and Robert took notes. In 1972 Seth's book was published as a full-scale, spirit-authored work bearing the title, *Seth Speaks: The Eternal Validity of the Soul*, written by Seth, yet transcribed and edited by Robert Butts. Robert added notes on the sidebar describing his wife's facial expressions and mannerisms while under the influence of her otherworldly author.

Seth Speaks is an extraordinary work, in which Seth comments upon science, religion, philosophy, the nature of reality, and ethics. In the years that followed, eight more increasingly complicated, Seth-dictated books were published. Their world-famous titles are:

The Nature of Personal Reality: A Seth Book (1974).

- *The Unknown Reality, Volume 1* (1977).

- *The Unknown Reality, Volume 2* (1979).

- *The Nature of the Psyche: Its Human Expression* (1979).

- *The Individual and the Nature of Mass Events: A Seth Book* (1981).

- *Dreams, "Evolution," and Value Fulfillment, Volumes 1 & 2* (1986).

- *The Magical Approach* (1995).

- *The Way Toward Health* (1997).

Interestingly enough, throughout this period Jane published many other books under her own name. Significantly, when one compares Jane's books with the Seth-dictated books, it's quite obvious that the writing styles and personalities reflected are clearly different. The Seth books *did not come from Jane Roberts*. The sessions, dictations, and notations by Robert Butts continued until Jane's health-related death on September 5, 1984. Seth's voice then ceased.

But his influence hasn't. In addition to the many Seth-dictated books, audio recordings of many Seth sessions before wondering psychologists and researchers were also taped, and they exist today. Because of the extraordinary and verifiable nature of these supernatural communications, boxes and boxes of Robert Butts' handwritten notes now permanently reside inside the prestigious Yale Archives in New Haven, Connecticut, where volunteers endeavor to commit Seth's words to a comprehensive computer database.

To date, over 7.5 million Seth books have sold worldwide, with translations in over a dozen languages. There is a "Seth Learning Center," myriads of Seth-related Web sites, and countless Internet blogs and discussion groups about "The Seth Material." The Seth Learning Center boldly declares, "Seth's empowering message literally launched the New Age Movement [in the

1960s]."[4] Even in our 21st century, The Seth Movement shows no signs of letting up. His teachings have been proclaimed as of equal or greater importance than those of Jesus Christ.

One skeptic-turned-believer wrote:

I first encountered The Seth Material on a rainy afternoon in the upper level stacks of the Towanda Public Library, in Pennsylvania. Earlier, in a local paper, I had seen a small write-up about a woman in Elmira, New York, who goes into trance and speaks as someone named Seth. "Yeah, right," I remember thinking.

Then that day in the library, my hand closed over a volume. I saw the title, shrugged, and checked it out. I had no idea of the ride I was about to embark upon.

At age 40, I was not totally unprepared for Seth. I had studied Rosicrucian monographs for nine years and, since my early twenties, had felt a keen interest in metaphysics and philosophy. Yet, I always had a skepticism about mediums and séances and things ectoplasmic.

I began reading. I learned of the coming of Seth into the lives of Jane Roberts and her husband Robert Butts. It was bemusing to follow the progress of two people who may well have been as skeptical as I. Well, how would you feel if suddenly some personality essence entity entered your body and proceeded to lecture? It's quite one thing to accept it in theory, but if it happened to me, I think it would scare me—well—witless.

I read on. I got past the mediumship thing and into the meat of the message. When I began to assimilate what Seth was saying, I no longer cared whether Ms. Roberts was getting the information from a disembodied spirit or her goldfish. The material, to me, was electrifying.

On one hand, it seemed hauntingly familiar. I found myself saying, "Of course, that's how it must be!" And "Yes, I seem to remember...." On the other hand, it took me a very long time to read The Seth Material (and every other Seth book). You don't speed read Seth! I would encounter a concept, read the paragraph over and over until I thought I understood it. Yet there was always a nagging feeling that I didn't, not completely, and I kept doing a Scarlett O'Hara: I'll think about it tomorrow.

All that was nearly thirty years ago. Since then I've purchased all of the Seth books and have read them many times. I will, as long as I continue to have a pulse, read them many times more. I once wrote to Robert Butts and told him that the Seth books were my easy answer to the question, what books would I take if shipwrecked. I only partially joke when I say they keep rewriting themselves between readings, offering more and more information as I become capable of comprehending it.

Has all this changed my life? Indeed! Once begun, the material became an inevitable path of study. It challenged, and often stripped away, many of my most ingrained beliefs, and expanded my consciousness so that my view of the world is forever altered. Did the Seth books offer a magic solution to all my problems? Of course not! Have they offered new insights on how to deal with them? Absolutely—but more as a by-product of what I consider to be the most fascinating, absorbing, and stimulating information on the nature of everything.

I find Seth to be fun. Like an early, beloved schoolteacher whose influence persists throughout our lives, Seth speaks with humor, compassion and patience. Seth is not a cult. Seth is not a religion. Seth does not proselytize. Seth teaches. If you start with The Seth Material—and I do recommend reading the books in the order in which they were written—there are more than a dozen more, each superb.

If I were asked to give a one-sentence description of all of Seth's material, I would quote my son who was brought up on it: "It's the highest distillation of common sense."[5]

Such testimonies can be easily multiplied. Today, Seth has millions of devout followers. Here are just a few quotes from internationally recognized spiritual leaders about the impact Seth has had on their personal lives and teaching:

The Seth books present an alternate map of reality with a new diagram of the psyche...useful to all explorers of consciousness.

—Deepak Chopra, M.D.,
author of *Ageless Body, Timeless Mind*[6]

Seth was one of my first metaphysical teachers. He remains a constant source of knowledge and inspiration in my life.

—Marianne Williamson,
author of *A Return to Love*[7]

The Nature of Personal Reality: A Seth Book had an important influence on my life and work. Seth's teachings provided one of the initial inspirations for writing *Creative Visualization.*

—Shakti Gawain,
author of *Creative Visualization*[8]

I would like to see the Seth books as required reading for anyone on their spiritual pathway. The amazing in-depth information in the

Seth books is as relevant today as it was in the early 70s when Jane Roberts first channeled this material.

—Louise Hay,
author of *You Can Heal Your Life*[9]

As you read Seth's words, you will gain more than just new ideas. Seth's energy comes through every page, energy that expands your consciousness and changes your thoughts about the nature of reality.

—Sanaya Roman,
author of *Living With Joy*[10]

Later we will examine some of Seth's teachings, but at this point it's enough to note the ongoing influence of this invisible entity that suddenly appeared in the 1960s in Elmira, New York. *This is not a fictitious story.* Similar to Dr. Gary E. Schwartz's research with Allison DuBois and others, "[Jane Roberts'] experience contains, in dramatic form, all of the earmarks of a genuine medium being reached and controlled from the Other Side," declared occult expert Tal Brooke, President of the Berkeley-based Spiritual Counterfeits Project.[11]

The majority of books, articles, and web sites dedicated to *The Seth Material* feature only glowing reports and testimonials about how wonderful Seth is. Even today—almost 50 years after Seth first "spoke" through an Ouija board—millions still praise American medium Jane Roberts and her insightful ghost.

But there's another side to this Seth story that usually goes unreported. It lies hidden, buried mostly within the deceased memory of Jane Roberts. But it exists. When one looks below the surface, frightening things bubbled up from inside that New York apartment which became a portal to another world. It's time to bring some of these things to light. Later we will remove Seth's mask entirely, uncovering his true identity.

Not long after the Ouija board first moved, in an attempt to verify his existence to Jane and Robert, Seth told those at the séance table to concentrate on Jane's arm. "One witness, Robert Butts, said that the hand began to change in appearance and resembled a paw. It gave Butts a very eerie feeling. He said that the hand became stubby and fat for a moment. Then it resumed its paw-like appearance. Then Seth told him to reach out and touch the hand. Butts cautiously touched Jane's hand. It felt very cold, wet, and clammy, and seemed unusually bumpy. Then Seth made the whole forepaw glow."[12] Remember how Montel Williams experienced a bone-chilling coldness when he stepped through Mary's ghost? Or how Allison DuBois' hands nearly freeze each time she is "holding hands with the Other Side"? Seth had a "cold, wet, and clammy" touch also.

After a few other bizarre antics, Jane and her husband became convinced that they had indeed encountered the supernatural. But soon another incident almost ended their newfound relationship with one who claimed to be so friendly. Jane "was in her bedroom, and became suddenly aware of a dark, looming figure menacing her. She had not previously believed in demons, but changed her mind when the attacker dragged her around and even bit her hand. Finally, the thing tried to kill her and she screamed."[13]

One would think Jane Roberts and Robert Butts would have trashed their Ouija board, but they didn't. During a subsequent session, Jane asked Seth to explain the event, which he was quick to do. He said the whole thing "was merely a projection of her [Jane's] mind, the energy of hidden fears," *not him*.[14] The "evil" that Jane imagined was just that, imaginary. It didn't exist. Somehow, Jane overcame her fears and kept going, completely trusting her otherworldly "friend."

If you do an Internet search for "Jane Roberts" and the "Seth Books," and then look at the book covers, they usually appear neat and attractive. The truth is, they've been given a face lift. The early edition of the first book, "*Seth Speaks* by Jane Roberts," shows an actual picture of Jane Roberts on the front cover that was taken during one of her trances. As I write this, I'm looking at that original book cover now—and it is ghastly! With the invisible Seth entity operating inside her, Jane's face is disfigured horribly.

When occult expert Tal Brooke first saw that same book cover in a bookstore, he later reflected:

> I stared at the gnarled face of Jane Roberts emerging from a purple paperback cover, contorting like a vampire in a Polish horror film. She had been photographed while "Seth" had taken over her body. I squinted my eyes in thought and looked off. Recalling my era in Egyptology, I said to myself, "Seth is the name of the Egyptian god of evil." Sure enough, when I checked it out in Webster's dictionary, it said: "Seth, n. an Egyptian god represented as having the head of a beast and a pointed snout. He was the brother of Osiris and the personification of physical evil and darkness, the adversary of good."[15]

To be fair, the name "Seth" also appears in the Bible, in the Book of Genesis. The biblical Seth was the third son of Adam and Eve who was born shortly after their first son, Cain, murdered their second son, Abel. In Genesis, "Seth" means, "one who had been appointed." Adam and Eve gave their third son this name because they believed their child was "appointed" by God, and that his birth was not an accident. The Scripture records:

And Adam knew his wife again, and she bore a son and named him Seth, "For God has appointed another seed for me instead of Abel [Eve said], *whom Cain killed." And as for Seth, to him also a son was born:*

and he named him Enosh. Then men began to call upon the name of the Lord (Genesis 4:25-26).

Demons in Disguise is not meant to be a scary book. Nevertheless, there are some frightening things happening in our world that need to be addressed *and exposed*. The spirit who identified himself as "Seth" claimed to be a good spirit, yet when he took over Jane Roberts' body, her face contorted horribly. He also made her hand look like a paw, which her husband said felt "cold, wet, and clammy." And what was that "thing" that attacked Jane in her bedroom? "It wasn't me," Seth replied smugly. "It was only a manifestation of Jane's inner fears." Was Seth telling the truth?

As I write this book, my wife Kristin and I have only one son (he is 28 months old), *and his name is Seth!* We didn't name him after Jane Roberts' spirit guide, but after the third son of Adam and Eve. Kristin and I like the verse that says that after the biblical Seth was born, "men began to call upon the name of the Lord." When we look at our son's happy face, we see innocence, childlike simplicity, and sweetness. When our little boy excitedly says to me, "Watch this, Daddy!" and then performs some childish trick, my heart soars with a joy only a parent can know. I always want my son's face to be radiant, and never horribly disfigured like that of Jane Roberts. I wonder what Jane's mother would say if she saw that book cover? If the Seth ghost reappeared in our day, I wouldn't want him possessing my kid. *Not on your life.*

You are about to discover that just as there are two very different Seths—the one who made Jane Roberts' face look gruesome, and the one mentioned in the Bible—even so are there two vastly different spiritual powers contending against each other on the Other Side. One is perfect, loving, and truly friendly. When it enters our bodies, it makes our faces glow. The other appears friendly, but it lies. The Book of Revelation says that these two antagonistic powers are now at war with each other and that this behind-the-scenes conflict will rage until the close of time.

Again, the goal of this book isn't to scare you, but to warn and enlighten you. Its ultimate purpose is to lead you into the arms of a supernatural power that genuinely loves you, and wants what's best for you.

And as you will soon see, our ability to discern the true nature of these opposing powers can be greatly enhanced by reading the very first book of the Bible, the Book of Genesis, and by understanding what it teaches about our Creator and about Adam, Eve, and the serpent.

Yes, *the serpent*.

Thousands of years ago, a ghost entered a snake.

That ghost still exists today.

ENDNOTES

1. Tal Brooke, *The Mystery of Death* (Berkeley, CA: End Run Publishing, 2001), 57.

2. Brooke, *The Mystery of Death*, 58.

3. Brooke, *The Mystery of Death*, 57.

4. See http://www.sethlearningcenter.org/.

5. A book review of *The Seth Material* by a man who calls himself, senja-su. Posted on Amazon.com. See http://www.amazon.com/Seth-Material-Jane-Roberts/dp/0971119805/sr=8-1/qid=1167354293/ref=pd_bbs_sr_1/104-9918651-7547920?ie=UTF8&s=books.

6. See http://www.sethlearningcenter.org/testimonials.html.

7. See http://www.sethlearningcenter.org/testimonials.html.

8. See http://www.sethlearningcenter.org/testimonials.html.

9. See http://www.sethlearningcenter.org/testimonials.html.

10. See http://www.sethlearningcenter.org/testimonials.html.

11. Brooke, *The Mystery of Death*, 56.

12. Brooke, *The Mystery of Death*, 57-58.

13. Brooke, *The Mystery of Death*, 58.

14. Brooke, *The Mystery of Death*, 58.

15. Brooke, *The Mystery of Death*, 55.

Chapter 5

IDENTIFYING
A FALLEN FOE

The devil hath power to assume a pleasing shape.

—William Shakespeare (1564-1616), *Hamlet*, Act 2, Scene 2

WHAT dwells beyond the veil? Psychics, paranormal researchers, clairvoyants, and modern mediums usually emphasize that in the invisible world the spirits of dead people roam freely. Hollywood producers often agree, as do increasing numbers within society at large. In her *New York Times* best-selling book, *Visits From the Afterlife*, Sylvia Browne states her conviction that there are literally "billions of spirits on The Other Side,"[1] including heavenly "spirits" of departed souls, earthbound "ghosts" who don't realize they're dead, personal "Spirit Guides," "Angels," and even animal spirits called "totems."[2]

In *Visits*, Browne also testifies, "It's literally true that I've read the Bible more times than I can count."[3] She calls the Bible, "that great book,"[4] and refers to "God,"[5] "the Holy Spirit,"[6] "Jesus,"[7] "the Holy Trinity,"[8] and her own "church"[9] where she regularly lectures before large audiences. "I'm sixty-six years old," Browne declares, "and I've never spent one instant doubting that there's life after death. ...God certainly doesn't doubt it, since He's the One who told us it's true in the first place, *and we take His Word for everything.*"[10]

Thus Sylvia Browne—one of the 21st century's most influential mediums—says she believes everything that is written in God's Book. So here's a key question: Does she agree with what the Bible teaches about evil? Does she believe there are sinister forces lurking beyond our five senses? This is where things become a bit murky. To be sure, Browne does affirm that a "dark side" exists that is inhabited by invisible "toxic dark entities"[11] bent on mischief and negativity. Labeling these harmful intelligences "terrorists in spirit form,"[12] she blames them for the many "psychic attacks" she and her global clientele have experienced throughout the years. In fact, Browne acknowledges that it was her spirit guide, Francine that first gave her the term "psychic attack."[13]

Here's another question: Do those "terrorists in spirit form" who sometimes initiate "psychic attacks" have a leader? In other words, is there one diabolic personality behind the scenes who is ultimately responsible for all the heartache, crime, chaos, and confusion now plaguing our world—such as "the devil"? Browne's answer is crystal clear: *No, there isn't.* No "mythical devil" inhabits the spirit world.[14] Browne's own Web site emphatically affirms that one of her core teachings is the belief that there is "*no fear, no guilt, no sin, no hell, and no Satan.*"[15] "Evil is a creation of humankind,"[16] she informs us, and nothing more. To Browne, all "toxic dark entities" are merely misguided human souls that have drifted away from "the light."

No fear, no guilt, no sin, no hell, and no satan.

This belief is common today, especially among the growing number of "professional mediums" who appear on TV talk shows and are interviewed on national radio programs. Because they don't believe in the existence of a distinct personality named "satan," or in his demons, they generally assume that whenever a spirit or ghost appears to them that looks like a dead person, talks like a dead person, acts like a dead person, and knows things that apparently only that dead person can know, then it must be the spirit of that dead person. Even if the talking entity is unfamiliar, if it speaks nice words and claims heavenly origin, modern mediums—and most other people—accept what they see at face value, without considering the possibility that they are being duped by some highly deceptive intelligence adept at the art of impersonation. In *Visits*, Sylvia Browne candidly reveals:

> Many of you know the story of my first one-on-one, clear-as-a-bell, no-way-around-it spirit encounter. I was eight years old, alone in my bed one night, when a glow of light cut through the darkness and the slightly vague form of a tall, slender woman with long black hair stepped toward me from the core of the light. "Don't be afraid," she said, "I come from God." I ran screaming to my grandma Ada, who calmly explained that I'd just received a visit from my Spirit Guide. Her name was Ilena, but I changed it to Francine for no apparent reason, and like all Spirit Guides, she's been my closest companion and advisor every minute of every day of my life this time around.[17]

Sylvia Browne's experience is similar to that of Allison DuBois, and many others, who have unexpectedly encountered spirits when they were mere children. "Ilena" announced to young Sylvia, "I come from God," and the girl and her grandmother believed this announcement. Because Ilena appeared wrapped in "a glow of light," doesn't this prove it was a good spirit? Not exactly. It only proves that Ilena *appeared* friendly.

On March 16, 2005, 32-year-old Scott Peterson was sentenced to death for murdering his pregnant wife, Laci. Before Laci's mysterious disappearance on Christmas Eve, 2005, Mr. Peterson also appeared friendly. He dutifully escorted Laci to regular doctor appointments and family outings. To many observers, Scott Peterson appeared to be a happy husband excited about becoming a daddy. During the murder trial, one of the jurists referred to the defendant as polite and courteous. Yet Scott Peterson's cordial exterior covered up the darkest heart. On April 14, 2003, Laci Peterson's nearly unrecognizable corpse washed up onto the shore of San Francisco Bay. The man had killed his own wife and baby.

It's time to begin examining what the Bible says about "satan," the master deceiver. Later we'll look at what it teaches about these "Four Ds": Demons, Death, the Dead, and talking to Dead People. Its message may surprise you.

But first, be aware that the concept of a personal devil is not just a Christian idea, but is recognized around the world. Even children, upon seeing a cartoonish image of a slender, reddish being with horns, a pitchfork, and a sly smile, will instantly remark, "There's the devil!" His picture appears on Red Devil Fireworks every Fourth of July. Kids wear devil costumes on Halloween. TV commercials depict him as a little red guy perched on your shoulder whispering temptation into your ear. "The devil made me do it!" is a popular slogan. Rock n' Roller Mick Jagger still bellows his hit song "Sympathy for the Devil" before enthralled audiences. Thus, even in our modern, hi-tech times, the devil still generates plenty of publicity.

Beliefs about "satan" vary widely, from the sober to the silly. Obviously, many reject the "personal devil" idea. Some think that Christian leaders—for the purpose of manipulating their followers into obeying the Church to avoid damnation—manufactured the entire notion. Many believe the term "satan" applies only to "evil" in general, or simply to the "dark side" of humanity. According to this view, "satan" is merely a symbol, concept, or principle, but not a person or intelligent being.

The question remains, *does a real devil exist?* Sylvia Browne doesn't think so. Neither do most psychics, clairvoyants, and mediums. What does the Bible say?

It's time to find out. The prophet Isaiah wrote:

How you are fallen from heaven,
O Lucifer, son of the morning!
How you are cut down to the ground,
You who weakened the nations!
For you have said in your heart:
"I will ascend into heaven,
I will exalt my throne above the stars of God;
I will also sit on the mount of the congregation
On the farthest sides of the north;
I will ascend above the heights of the clouds,
I will be like the Most High."
Yet you shall be brought down to Sheol [Hell],
To the lowest depths of the Pit (Isaiah 14:12-15).

This passage describes a *personality*, not a principle, whose original name was "lucifer," which means, "light bearer." Isaiah wrote that lucifer's home was in "heaven," but that he has "fallen." Although not fully explained, the reason for his fall is that pride developed in his heart. Lucifer inappropriately aspired to "be like the Most High"—to usurp the place of God Almighty. The result was his eviction from realms of glory. In a parallel passage, the prophet Ezekiel wrote:

You were the seal of perfection,
Full of wisdom and perfect in beauty.
You were in Eden, the garden of God;
Every precious stone was your covering:
The sardius, topaz, and diamond,
Beryl, onyx, and jasper,
Sapphire, turquoise, and emerald with gold.
The workmanship of your timbrels and pipes
Was prepared for you on the day you were created.

You were the anointed cherub who covers;
I established you;
You were on the holy mountain of God;
You walked back and forth in the midst of fiery stones.
You were perfect in your ways from the day you were created,
Till iniquity was found in you...
Therefore I cast you as a profane thing
Out of the mountain of God... (Ezekiel 28:12-16).

Again, this is a description of a personality—not a principle—who originally was "full of wisdom and perfect in beauty." Some scholars apply Isaiah 14:12-15 and Ezekiel 28:12-16 to a human being; but this is incorrect. No normal human being was "perfect in [his] ways from the day [he] was created, till iniquity was found in [him]." This cannot apply to any earthly individual.

Prior to his fall, Ezekiel identified this personality as "the anointed cherub who covers." This description is highly significant, for in the Bible the word "cherub" applies to *angels*, not to humans. In Old Testament times, God told His people to construct a sacred temple, which contained a sacred room called "the Most Holy Place," inside of which was a golden box called "the ark" in which was placed the Ten Commandments. On top of the ark rested a golden lid called "the mercy seat" on which sat two golden angels called cherubs. The Lord commanded Moses:

*And you shall make **two cherubim of gold**; of hammered work you shall make them at the two ends of the mercy seat. Make one cherub at one end, and the other cherub at the other end; you shall make the cherubim at the two ends of it of one piece with the mercy seat. **And the cherubim shall stretch out their wings above**, covering the mercy seat with their wings, and they shall face one another; the faces of the cherubim shall be toward the mercy seat* (Exodus 25:18-20, emphasis added).

The Most Holy Place represented in miniature the heavenly headquarters of the King of the Universe. The ark represented God's throne; the Ten Commandments, His Law; the golden lid, His mercy; and the two golden cherubim, the angelic host created to carry out His will. When Ezekiel called lucifer "the anointed cherub who covers," this is vital information that lucifer was originally a highly exalted angel beside God's throne. "You were perfect in your ways from the day you were created," the prophet wrote. "Till iniquity was found in you."

Again, this cannot apply to any man, or to some sort of generic evil principle. Such an interpretation perverts the prophet's words. Instead, Ezekiel is describing a magnificent angel who turned against his Maker. And once again, just like in the Isaiah text, Ezekiel pinpoints the root cause of this angelic apostasy as a proud heart. Finally God declared, "Therefore I cast you as a profane thing out of the mountain of God" (Ezek. 28:16). Self-centered pride in the presence of God Almighty can't be tolerated.

After his expulsion from Heaven, lucifer's name was changed to "satan," which means, "the adversary" (see Luke 10:18). Although his fall occurred thousands of years ago, the Bible is crystal clear that this diabolical entity still exists. The New Testament calls him:

- "the devil" (Matt. 4:1).

- "the tempter" (Matt. 4:3).

- "the evil one" (Matt. 6:13).

- "Beelzebub, the ruler of the demons" (Matt. 12:24).

- "a murderer from the beginning" (John 8:44).

- "a liar and the father of it" (John 8:44).

- "the ruler of this world" (John 14:30).

- "the prince of the power of the air" (Eph. 2:2).

- "your adversary the devil" (1 Pet. 5:8).

- "the wicked one" (1 John 3:12).

- "that serpent of old" (Rev. 12:9).

One biblical scene that strikingly illustrates satan's individuality, personality, and intelligence is the account of Jesus Christ's temptation in the wilderness. The Book of Matthew records:

Then Jesus was led up by the Spirit into the wilderness to be tempted by the devil. And when He had fasted forty days and forty nights, afterward He was hungry. Now when the tempter came to Him, he said, "If You are the Son of God, command that these stones become bread." But He answered and said, "It is written, 'Man shall not live by bread alone, but by every word that proceeds from the mouth of God.'" Then the devil took Him up into the holy city, set Him on the pinnacle of the temple, and said to Him, "If You are the Son of God, throw Yourself down. For it is written: 'He shall give His angels charge over you,' and, 'In their hands they shall bear you up, Lest you dash your foot against a stone.'" Jesus said to him, "It is written again, 'You shall not tempt the Lord your God.'" Again, the devil took Him up on an exceedingly high mountain, and showed Him all the kingdoms of the world and their glory. And he said to Him, "All these things I will give You if You will fall down and worship me." Then Jesus said to him, "Away with you, Satan! For it is written, 'You shall worship the Lord your God, and Him only you shall serve.'" Then the devil left Him, and behold, angels came and ministered to Him (Matthew 4:1-11).

This section should not be rationalized away. Jesus Christ was alone in the wilderness when a distinct voice whispered softly from the Other Side. Matthew says that this communication came from "the devil." Three times "the tempter" sought to seduce Christ away from His loyalty to God, yet three times he was steadfastly repulsed. A titanic struggle—unknown by the surrounding world—raged in the Judean Desert.

After each temptation, Christ quoted Scripture as His defense. In his second temptation, satan quoted Scripture too, but with deceptive subtlety. The original verse the devil quoted came from Psalm 91:11-12. If you look up that original passage, you will discover that satan quoted most of it, but he left out six words. Then he used the entire passage to tempt Jesus to do his bidding. This shows that the devil *knows the Bible*, can quote it, and pervert it. This should place us on our guard and impress us with the need to study God's Book thoroughly to know what it really says, instead of accepting what others claim it says.

In *Visits From the Afterlife*, Sylvia Browne declared, "We take His [God's] Word for everything."[18] This is a bizarre statement considering her public stance that there is "No fear, no guilt, no sin, no hell, *and no Satan.*" Here Browne clearly contradicts the Bible. The devil does exist. He is both brilliant and seductive. That's what the Bible says. As we've already seen, Browne also reported:

I was eight years old, alone in my bed one night, when a glow of light cut through the darkness and the slightly vague form of a tall, slender woman with long black hair stepped toward me from the core of the light. "Don't be afraid," she said, "I come from God."[19]

Because this spirit appeared within "a glow of light" and claimed heavenly origin, the young Sylvia believed it. I wish the older Sylvia would believe something else—what the Bible really teaches about the devil. If she did, verses like this would become an alarming wake-up call:

And no wonder! For Satan himself transforms himself into an angel of light (2 Corinthians 11:14).

The devil is smart. He can easily appear as "an angel of light." As you will discover in the next chapter, *so can his demons.*

ENDNOTES

1. Sylvia Browne, *Visits From the Afterlife: The Truth About Hauntings, Spirits, and Reunions With Lost Loved Ones* (London: New American Library, a division of Penguin books, 2003), 38.

2. Browne, *Visits*, 39-40.

3. Browne, *Visits*, 57.

4. Browne, *Visits*, 57.

5. Browne, *Visits*, 26.

6. Browne, *Visits*, 214.

7. Browne, *Visits*, 6.

8. Browne, *Visits*, 63.

9. Browne, *Visits*, 210.

10. Browne, *Visits*, xiv, emphasis added.

11. Browne, *Visits*, 209.

12. Browne, *Visits*, 213.

13. Browne, *Visits*, 212.

14. Browne, *Visits*, 5.

15. Taken from Sylvia Browne's web site. See http://www.novus.org/home/index.cfm.

16. Browne, *Visits*, 5.

17. Browne, *Visits*, 43.

18. Browne, *Visits*, xiv.

19. Browne, *Visits*, 43.

Chapter 6

"MY NAME IS LEGION"

Demons don't play by the rules. They lie and they cheat and they stab in the back.

—Alan Grant, Scottish Comic Book Writer (1949-)

THE Book of Revelation is the greatest book on prophecy ever written. Since the time of its origin in A.D. 96, it has attracted more readers than the writings of the world's most famous psychics—Nostradamus, Edgar Cayce, Madame Blavatsky, Arthur Ford, Jeanne Dixon, Uri Geller, John Edward, James Van Praagh, Allison DuBois, and Sylvia Browne—combined. Lifting the veil from an unseen world, it describes a Great War fought eons ago, not on earth, but in the courts above.

And war broke out in heaven: Michael and his angels fought with the dragon; and the dragon and his angels fought, but they did not prevail, nor was a place found for them in heaven any longer. So the great dragon was cast out, that serpent of old, called the Devil and Satan, who *deceives the whole world; he was cast to the earth, **and his angels were cast out with him*** (Revelation 12:7-9, emphasis added).

Did you catch that? War erupted in Heaven, satan was "cast to the earth, and his angels were cast out with him." Thus satan was not the only one penalized for an inexcusable act of rebellion. "His angels" were cast out with him.

"Angels" inhabit the Other Side. According to the Bible, angels are a special order of heavenly beings created by God to carry out His plans. They have never been, are not now, nor shall they ever be human like us. They're not the dead, nor the spirits of the dead. Angels are different and unique. And based on Revelation 12:7-9, there are now two distinct classes of them—good ones and bad ones. The good ones are those who remained loyal to their Maker in the Great War, whereas the bad ones are those who allied themselves with lucifer and suffered the consequences. Like uncooperative tenants in an apartment complex, they were all evicted from their heavenly home. Where did they go? The Bible is clear. Satan was "cast to the *earth*, and his angels were cast out with him" (Rev. 12:9).

How many loyal angels still remain on God's side? No one knows for sure, but there are myriads of them. The writer of the Book of Revelation reported:

*Then I looked, and I heard the voice of many angels around the throne, the living creatures, and the elders; **and the number of them was ten thousand times ten thousand, and thousands of thousands*** (Revelation 5:11, emphasis added).

If we do the math—10,000 x 10,000, plus thousands of thousands—that's a lot! From Genesis (the first book in the Bible) to Revelation (the grand finale), the existence, power, intelligence, and ministration of holy angels is repeatedly described. Here's a quick list of some of their activities, missions, and duties (past, present, and future):

- Holy angels guard and protect us (see Ps. 91:11).

- Holy angels minister to those who will inherit salvation (see Heb. 1:7,14).

- Holy angels bring messages from God (see Luke 1:13-19).

- Holy angels can appear in human form (see Gen. 19:1-11; Heb. 13:1-2).

- Holy angels sometimes announce significant events (see Luke 1:26-38).

- Holy angels rejoice when sinners repent (see Luke 15:10).

- Holy angels minister to those who are tempted (see Matt. 4:11).

- Holy angels bring strength during times of temptation (see Luke 22:43).

- Holy angels announced that Jesus Christ had risen from the dead (see Matt. 28:1-7).

- Holy angels explained to Jesus Christ's disciples the truth about His ascension and second coming (see Acts 1:9-11).

- Holy angels will accompany Jesus Christ when He returns to earth (see Matt. 24:30-31).

- Holy angels will separate the righteous from the wicked at the end of the world (see Matt. 13:40-42).

Many more Scriptures could be quoted. Here is one of my favorite passages describing the activity of good angels, "The angel of the Lord encamps all around those who fear Him, and delivers them" (Ps. 34:7). This shows that holy angels constantly hover "all around" God's people. Unseen by human eyes, they pitch camp and provide protection and deliverance. Why do we need such intervention? The answer should be obvious by now: *because of the evil angels.*

The angels who sided with lucifer also inhabit the Other Side, and they are working tirelessly just beyond our limited human vision. Although they usually remain invisible to the naked eye, they're as real as your legs, arms, hands, and feet. The Bible refers to these fallen fiends as:

- "unclean spirits" (Mark 6:7).

- "deceiving spirits" (1 Tim. 4:1).

- "principalities and powers" (Eph. 6:12).

- "rulers of the darkness of this age" (Eph. 6:12).

- "spiritual hosts of wickedness in heavenly places" (Eph. 6:12).

- "the angels that sinned" (2 Pet. 2:4).

- "the spirits of devils" (Rev. 16:14).

Lucifer's fallen angelic comrades are also called "demons" (see 1 Cor. 10:20). Merriam-Webster's Online Dictionary defines "demon" as "an evil spirit."[1] Liberal scholars often rationalize away the existence of demons, just like they deny satan's existence; but an honest evaluation of scriptural evidence disproves their theory. Perhaps the most striking example of the existence, intelligence, and malicious power of demonic entities is found in the Book of Mark, chapter 5:

Then they came to the other side of the sea, to the country of the Gadarenes. And when He [Jesus Christ] had come out of the boat, immediately there met Him out of the tombs a man with an unclean spirit, who had his dwelling among the tombs; and no one could bind him, not even with chains, because he had often been bound with shackles and chains. And the chains had been pulled apart by him, and the shackles broken in pieces; neither could anyone tame him. And always, night and day, he was in the mountains and in the tombs, crying out and cutting himself with stones. When he saw Jesus from afar, he ran and worshiped Him. And he cried out with a loud voice and said, "What have I to do with You, Jesus, Son of the Most High God? I implore You by God that You do not torment me." For He said to him, "Come out of the man, unclean spirit!" Then He asked him, "What is your name?" And he answered, saying, "My name is Legion; for we are many." Also he begged Him earnestly that He would not send them out of the country. Now a large herd of swine was feeding there near the mountains. So all the demons begged Him, saying, "Send us to the swine, that we may enter them." And at once Jesus gave them permission. Then the unclean spirits went out and entered the swine (there were about two thousand); and the herd ran violently down the steep place into the sea, and drowned in the sea. So those who fed the swine fled, and they told it in the city and in the country. And they went out to see what it was that had happened. Then they came to Jesus, and saw the one who had been demon-possessed and had the legion, sitting and clothed and in his right mind. And they were afraid. And those who saw it told them how it happened to him who had been demon-possessed, and about the swine. Then they began to plead with Him to depart from their region. And when He got into the boat, he who had been demon-possessed begged Him that he might be with Him. However, Jesus did not permit him, but said to him, "Go home to your friends, and tell them what great things the Lord has done for you, and how He has had compassion on you." And he departed and began to proclaim in Decapolis all that Jesus had done for him; and all marveled (Mark 5:1-20).

Just like Christ's encounter with satan in the Judean Desert reveals the existence of a real devil, even so does Mark 5:1-20 demonstrate the activity of real demons. Jesus and His disciples had just stepped onto shore from a boat, when a wild-eyed insane man with "an unclean spirit" lurched toward them from out of a cemetery. "Only his thoughts were unclean," some may suggest. "Real demons don't exist." But the rest of the account reveals otherwise.

Confronted with the spectacle of a naked, drooling specimen of humanity, Jesus looked beneath the surface and discerned the presence of the demonic. Without a trace of fear, Christ demanded, "What is your name?" When the unfortunate man opened his mouth to reply, another voice spoke through his vocal cords, saying, "My name is Legion; for we are many."

"A perfect case of mental illness," skeptics might maintain. "The notion of real demons possessing real people is fit for the Dark Ages!" But the Bible teaches otherwise. Noticing a large herd of pigs grazing peacefully on a nearby hillside, "Legion" requested, "Send us to the swine, that we may enter them." Jesus gave them permission. Faster than a child can say "boo!" one of the strangest events in history occurred. Two thousand unsuspecting animals suddenly jerked violently, and then rushed madly toward the precipice of a cliff. Something supernatural had entered their bodies and was now catapulting them toward the dark waters of the Sea of Galilee. Even their natural wills to survive couldn't save them. "The herd ran violently down the steep place into the sea, and drowned in the sea."

These details exclude the possibility that the insane man's problem was merely psychological illness, for the scene shifts from one two-legged madman to 2,000 four-legged animals. There's only one logical explanation for what happened to those pigs. *Legion did it.* In New Testament times, a "legion" was a division of troops in the Roman army. How many troops composed a legion? Here's the answer:

A Roman legion was an infantry unit consisting of heavily armed soldiers, equipped with shields, armor, helmets, spears and swords. In the early republic, the strength of a legion was about 3,000 men; there were 4,800 legionaries in the days of Julius Caesar; the twenty-five legions that defended the empire during the reign of Augustus counted more than 5,000 soldiers.[2]

Roman legions consisted of between 3,000 to 5,000 troops. We know that at least 2,000 demons inhabited the lunatic's body because that's how many pigs drowned in the sea. Everything fits, if you take the account at face value. When Jesus asked the madman, "What is your name?" He knew what He was up against. The eerie reply, "My name is Legion; for we are many," shows that lucifer's angels can enter human bodies, control human vocal cords, and speak through human lips. The demon's request, "Send us to the swine," reveals that these invisible entities are intelligent and calculating. They knew that the destruction of the pigs would result in their keepers wanting Jesus to leave the region, which is precisely what happened.

After the pigs drowned, "Then they [the keepers] began to plead with Him to depart from their region." So Jesus "got into the boat" and left. Although demons have no power to manipulate the Son of God, they still seek to coordinate circumstances. Jesus allowed this. He never forces Himself upon us, and He won't remain where He is not wanted. The demons accomplished their goal.

A close analysis of Mark 5:1-20 reveals these ten salient points about demons:

1. They exist as distinct personalities.
2. They can possess both human beings and animals.
3. They have minds.
4. They can think.
5. They can talk.
6. They are organized.
7. They have superhuman strength.
8. They can move invisibly through the air from place to place.
9. They are destructive.
10. They are subject to the authority of Jesus Christ.

Those who witnessed these remarkable events beheld a living testimony of the mercy, goodness, and power of the "Savior of the world" (see 1 John 4:14). An unfortunate man was demon-possessed, uncontrollable, running around without clothes, and dripping blood from self-inflicted sores. He had become a terror to the region. After meeting Jesus, however, he sat quietly before them, "clothed and in his right mind." If someone were to ask this man after his deliverance, "Do you believe real demons exist?" unquestionably his answer would have been, "Yes, they were inside my head!" The floating carcasses of 2,000 pigs bore witness to the facts. But because of the superior power of Jesus Christ, this man was now "in his right mind." He knew the truth. *So should we.*

In the New Testament, Jesus Christ taught that at the conclusion of human history He will sadly announce to unsaved sinners, "Depart from Me, you cursed, into the everlasting fire prepared for *the devil and his angels*" (Matt. 25:41, emphasis added). Jesus Christ affirms the existence of satan and his angels. He witnessed their fall from Heaven. He drove them from the body of a crazy man. He watched them destroy 2,000 pigs. And in Matthew 25:41, He clearly taught that at the end of the world, "the devil and his angels," and those who follow them, will reap the inevitable consequences of sin.

Satan, fallen angels, Jesus Christ, and loyal angels—they all inhabit the Other Side. So does a heavenly Presence called "the Spirit of truth" whose work is to guide us into "all truth" (see John 16:13). What about the ghosts of dead people? Are they there, too?

Keep reading. The answer is less than two minutes away.

ENDNOTES

1. See http://www.merriam-webster.com/dictionary/demon.

2. See http://www.livius.org/le-lh/legio/legions.htm.

Chapter 7

DEARLY DEPARTED DELUSIONS

Nothing in all the world is more dangerous than sincere ignorance and conscientious stupidity.

—Martin Luther King Jr. (1929-1968), *Strength to Love*, 1963

MODERN psychics and professional mediums who appear as guests on national radio and TV talk shows often refer to God, the Bible, and even to Jesus Christ in their interviews while relaying their "messages" to a confused, hurting, mixed-up public. Now, I certainly believe in God, and I'm all for quoting Scripture, but it's important to quote God's Book correctly—especially when it comes to what it says about conversing with dead people. What does it say?

Over 3,000 years ago, God delivered approximately two million Israelites from Egyptian slavery, led them through a desolate wilderness, and then brought them to the edge of Canaan, the Promised Land. Before bringing them into the territory that was to become their new home, God warned

Israel about certain practices that were common among the inhabiting nations. Notice carefully His counsel through Moses:

> *When you come into the land which the Lord your God is giving you, you shall not learn to follow the abominations of those nations. There shall not be found among you anyone who makes his son or his daughter pass through the fire, or who practices witchcraft, or a soothsayer, or one who interprets omens, or a sorcerer, or one who conjures spells,* **or a medium, or a spiritist, or one who calls up the dead.** *For all who do these things are an abomination to the Lord, and because of these abominations the Lord your God drives them out from before you. You shall be blameless before the Lord your God* (Deuteronomy 18:9-13, emphasis added).

This passage should be carefully considered. God's people were about to "come into the land," but that territory was full of dangers. Many nations already dwelt there, and they were practicing things that God knew were not only perilous, but also tempting. So to avoid any misunderstanding, He listed them distinctly, one by one, and then commanded His people to steer clear of them. Here's the list of forbidden activities found in Deuteronomy 18:9-13:

- Child sacrifice
- Witchcraft
- Soothsaying
- Interpreting omens
- Sorcery
- Casting spells
- Mediumship
- Spiritualism
- Calling up the dead

All of these ancient activities are being practiced today, and many are even being promoted in products sold at Wal-Mart and other popular stores. In my other book, *Exposing Harry Potter and Witchcraft: The Menace Behind the Magic*, I have already written about "witchcraft," "sorcery," and "spells," so I won't revisit these here. The targeted focus of *Demons in Disguise* is the last three: being "a medium, or a spiritist, or one who calls up the dead."

Obviously, the word *medium* remains a contemporary term, as it has now become the title of a popular NBC television series. Allison DuBois, James Van Praagh, John Edward, Carla Mae, Sylvia Browne, and Lisa Williams are all living, practicing, modern-day mediums. The word *spiritist* is essentially interchangeable with *medium*, although it isn't as widely used today. A spiritist is a person who communicates with spirits. This practice is also called Spiritualism. "Calling up the dead" is what mediums and spiritists do. Some Bible translations, like the King James Version or the Revised Standard Version, use the term "necromancy" instead of saying "one who calls up the dead" to describe the same practice. The Merriam-Webster Online Dictionary defines "necromancy" as:

Function: *noun*

1: conjuration of the spirits of the dead for purposes of magically revealing the future or influencing the course of events.[1]

The key point is that Deuteronomy 18:11 completely forbids being "a medium, or a spiritist, or one who calls up the dead." The clear message of the text is: "Don't be a medium, and don't talk to dead people!" And this warning applies to those who choose such a profession (mediums and spiritists) and to the practice itself (of seeking to contact dead people), no matter how honest or conscientious either the mediums or their followers may be about the ethics of their endeavors. Sincerity isn't the issue. The Scripture emphatically states:

For all who do these things are an abomination to the Lord, and because of these abominations the Lord your God drives them out from before you. You shall be blameless before the Lord your God (Deuteronomy 18:12-13, emphasis added).

The word *abomination* isn't a neutral word, nor can it easily be dismissed. One Bible dictionary lists these three definitions for "abomination":

Abomination (*n.*) The feeling of extreme disgust and hatred; abhorrence; detestation; loathing; as, he holds tobacco in abomination.

Abomination (*n.*) That which is abominable; anything hateful, wicked, or shamefully vile; an object or state that excites disgust and hatred; a hateful or shameful vice; pollution.

Abomination (*n.*) A cause of pollution or wickedness.[2]

You get the point. When Moses wrote that "a medium, or a spiritist, or one who calls up the dead" is an "*abomination* to the Lord," he was communicating in the strongest language possible where God stands in this matter. "Abominations" are things that are utterly detestable, hateful, vile, disgusting, and abhorrent to a pure and holy God. If this language sounds too strong, don't blame me. I didn't write Deuteronomy 18. Moses did. And Moses was simply revealing what "the Lord" thinks about trying to talk to dead people.

Has God changed His mind? And if not, why not? What's wrong with trying to contact one's deceased grandma anyway? Is God hard-hearted, narrow-minded, and bigoted? Is He unreasonably restricting those who have lost loved ones from being comforted by the Other Side? And what about well-meaning spiritual teachers? Isn't He being grossly unfair to them as well?

The truthful answer is no, not in the slightest degree. The more we discern what the Bible teaches about this topic, the more we will realize that God's motives are pure and that His goal is to *protect* all of us—including mediums themselves—from getting hurt, from hurting others, and from being deceived by malicious spirits that inhabit the invisible realm. Do parents speak strongly to their children about playing the street? Is such language justified?

Of course it is. Parents want to protect their kids. The same is true of our loving Creator, and of His firm language in Deuteronomy 18. His ultimate goal is to shield us from fallen angels, and from the disastrous consequences of opening up our hearts to their presence, power, teaching, and influence. Speaking of God, the Bible says, "He cares for you" (1 Pet. 5:7). Our Creator loves us more than we realize.

Even though the word *demon* isn't found in Deuteronomy 18, there are plenty of other Scriptures that clearly connect *talking to the dead with the demonic*. As the Israelites approached the Promised Land, their route took them through the region of Moab just east of Canaan. Pitching camp at a place called "Acacia Grove," they unexpectedly encountered an enticing, yet deadly enemy.

Now Israel remained in Acacia Grove, and the people began to commit harlotry with the women of Moab. They invited the people to the sacrifices of their gods, and the people ate and bowed down to their gods. So Israel was joined to Baal of Peor, and the anger of the Lord was aroused against Israel (Numbers 25:1-2).

The Moabites worshiped a pagan deity named "Baal," and many other gods. As word spread among them that the Israelites were passing through their territory, their leaders began laying plans to seduce Israel to participate in their idolatrous practices. Quietly, and unnoticed at first, beautiful Moabite women crept into the Israelite camp to tempt them into sin. The strategy worked. God's people yielded to feminine charms, and soon these Moabites tempters "invited the people [of Israel] to the sacrifices of their gods, and the people ate and bowed down to their gods." Thus Israel's loyalty shifted from the Creator of heaven and earth to pagan deities.

Who were these "gods"? Significantly, the Moabites believed their gods were actually their own tribal heroes who after death had simply passed over to the Other Side. That's why, although Numbers 25:2 says that at "Baal of

Peor" the Israelites ate "the sacrifices of their [the Moabite] gods," the Book of Psalms later records that at the exact same location the Israelites really "*ate sacrifices made to the dead.*" The Psalmist wrote:

> *They* [the Israelites] *joined themselves also to Baal of Peor, and ate sacrifices **made to the dead*** (Psalm 106:28, emphasis added).

This fact is established by comparing Numbers 25:2 with Psalm 106:28 that the ancient Moabites believed "the dead" had become "their gods." Now here's the most important part. Just a few verses after Psalm 106:28, the Psalmist goes one step further by stating that the Israelites, by eating food offered to Moabite "gods"—which they believed to be their "dead"—were actually *worshiping demons* without realizing it. Here are all three passages, so you can see the connections:

> *They* [the Moabites] *invited the people* [the Israelites] *to **the sacrifices of their gods**, and the people ate and bowed down to their gods. So Israel was joined to Baal of Peor, and the anger of the Lord was aroused against Israel* (Numbers 25:1-2, emphasis added).

> *They* [the Israelites] *joined themselves also to Baal of Peor, and ate **sacrifices made to the dead*** (Psalm 106:28, emphasis added).

> *They* [the Israelites] *served their* [Moabite] *idols [at Baal of Peor], which became a snare to them. They even* [the next step] *sacrificed their sons and their daughters **to demons*** (Psalm 106:36-37, emphasis added).

Thus the Moabite "gods," which they believed to be their "dead," were really "demons"—but of this both the Moabites and the Israelites were ignorant. The horrific practice of sacrificing "their sons and their daughters" to these gods-who-were-demons was common in those savage days. The same practice is referred to in Deuteronomy 18 where Moses warned against "anyone who makes his son or his daughter pass through the fire" (see Deut. 18:10). Yet although Moses plainly warned about it, at "Baal of Peor" the Israelites did it; and it all started with Moabite temptresses. Under the influence of wily female seducers, Israel steadily progressed from snuggling up with Moabite women, to eating food sacrificed to Moabite dead people, to finally murdering their own children on bloodstained Moabite altars. And all the while, behind the scenes, invisible fallen angels pulled the strings. It is especially these demonic forces that our loving Creator is concerned about.

In the New Testament, the apostle Paul also identified evil angels as the behind-the-scenes recipients of misguided pagan worship. With penetrating insight, Paul lifted the curtain and declared:

> *The things which the Gentiles sacrifice they sacrifice* **to demons** *and not to God, and I do not want you to have* **fellowship with demons** (1 Corinthians 10:20, emphasis added).

"Fellowship with demons" concerned Paul greatly. To have fellowship with a demon means that a human being is ignorantly holding communion with a fallen angel—that a relationship has developed with a representative of the devil. "I do not want you to have fellowship with demons," Paul told his converts. This is the true motivation behind his counsel, and it is also the real reason why God warned His ancient people in Deuteronomy 18 not to talk to dead people. Again, our loving Creator is seeking to protect us from invisible, hostile personalities.

The New King James Version of the Bible uses the word "medium" in Deuteronomy 18:11, as do many other translations (NASB, RSV, and NIV), yet some translations (KJV, ASV) replace "medium" with this phrase: "a consulter with *familiar spirits*." Essentially, the two are synonymous. A "medium" is a person who consults "familiar spirits," and "familiar spirits" are the spirits that guide, direct, provide information to, and that sometimes possess mediums.

Earlier we discovered how it came about that Allison DuBois—the inspiration behind NBC's "Medium" series—first decided to contact afterlife researcher Gary Schwartz at the University of Arizona. DuBois candidly acknowledged:

> *My guides* told me that I was to be part of Dr. Schwartz's research and that I had to contact him. *My guides* never steer me wrong....[3]

Similarly, Sylvia Browne also confessed:

> I was eight years old, alone in my bed one night, when a glow of light cut through the darkness and the slightly vague form of a tall, slender woman with long black hair stepped toward me from the core of the light. "Don't be afraid," she said, "I come from God." I ran screaming to my grandma Ada, who calmly explained that I'd just received *a visit from my Spirit Guide.* Her name was Ilena, but I changed it to Francine for no apparent reason, and like all Spirit Guides, she's been my closest companion and advisor every minute of every day of my life this time around.[4]

Thus DuBois and Browne both acknowledge that they have personal "spirit guides" that constantly direct their lives. These guides tell them what to do and where to go. In other words, they are thinking, calculating, non-physical entities. They also provide details—which are often amazingly accurate—about the living and the dead. Sylvia Browne's "spirit guide," a ghost she calls "Francine," is her "closest companion and advisor." The Bible calls these guides *"familiar spirits,"* the invisible companions of mediums and spiritists.

"Familiar spirits" are often mentioned in God's Book, but always in a negative sense. Read below and see for yourself. The Lord commanded the Israelites to:

*Give no regard to mediums and **familiar spirits**; do not seek after them, to be defiled by them: I am the Lord your God* (Leviticus 19:31, emphasis added).

A few verses later, God warned again:

*And the person who turns to mediums and **familiar spirits**, to prostitute himself with them, I will set My face against that person and cut him off from his people* (Leviticus 20:6, emphasis added).

Communication with familiar spirits was considered to be such a serious offense in Bible days that it even merited the death penalty. The Lord declared:

*A man or a woman who is a medium, **or who has familiar spirits**, shall surely be put to death; they shall stone them with stones. Their blood shall be upon them* (Leviticus 20:27, emphasis added).

Such strong warnings may seem unfair and harsh to our modern ears. And they would be, if the "familiar spirits" referred to in these passages were truly who they claim to be—friendly advisors and benefactors. But what if they aren't? What if they are really highly intelligent, masterfully deceptive, and even ruthless personalities whose secret agenda is to mislead and destroy both the mediums themselves (who have been duped by their wiles) and their clients? Then God's solemn warnings would make a great deal of sense.

In Old Testament times, an Israelite king named Manasseh became infamous for his idolatry, apostasy, and sin. As part of his downward spiral,

Manasseh slipped into the very practices God condemned so strongly in Leviticus and Deuteronomy. The Book of Second Kings provides this salient recap:

> *Manasseh was twelve years old when he became king, and he reigned fifty-five years in Jerusalem. His mother's name was Hephzibah. And he did evil in the sight of the Lord, according to the abominations of the nations whom the Lord had cast out before the children of Israel. For he rebuilt the high places which Hezekiah his father had destroyed; he raised up altars for Baal, and made a wooden image, as Ahab king of Israel had done; and he worshiped all the host of heaven and served them. He also built altars in the house of the Lord, of which the Lord had said, "In Jerusalem I will put My name." And he built altars for all the host of heaven in the two courts of the house of the Lord* (2 Kings 21:1-5).

Notice the culmination of his multifaceted departure from His Maker:

> *Also he made his son pass through the fire, practiced soothsaying, used witchcraft, and* **consulted spiritists and mediums.** *He did much evil in the sight of the Lord, to provoke Him to anger* (2 Kings 21:6, emphasis added).

Consulting spiritists and mediums is identified as being "evil in the sight of the Lord," and as something that "provoke[s] Him to anger." How unfair and harsh! But wait a minute. Think about it this way. What if you were the parent of a little boy and girl whom you loved with all your heart, and then you discovered, through an inside "tip," that there was a serial killer who was developing a well-thought-out plan to seduce, molest, and kill your kids? And what if you also learned that this evil person not only worked at the Day Care Center where you regularly drop off your children, but had recently applied to become their baby-sitter? Wouldn't *you* be horrified and angry too? Just talk to the parents and relatives of Laci Peterson if you have any question about how you would feel.

As the father of a two-year-old boy, I hate to write about these kinds of things. I wish they didn't happen; but they do. Our world is filled with widows, orphans, heartbroken parents, and other victims of satanic cruelty. Just read the newspaper headlines, or watch CNN, if you have the stomach for it. The awful reality is that real evil not only exists, but that it is both smart and calculating.

If a loving God rules in the heavens, how did we get into this mess in the first place? Where did it all start? This dilemma is one of the most baffling issues facing humanity today. Endless opinions exist, but the Bible gives only one definitive answer: The root problem is *lucifer and fallen angels.* And according to the Scriptures, one of the most effective ways that these invisible legions of darkness find direct access to unsuspecting human beings is by appearing as "familiar spirits"—the ghosts of dead people. Think about it. If you were the real God of all creation, and if you understood these matters perfectly, wouldn't you speak strongly against "familiar spirits" in your Book? I rest my case.

In contrast to the wicked actions of King Manasseh are the righteous deeds of King Josiah. This is what Josiah did:

> *Moreover Josiah put away those who consulted mediums and spiritists, the household gods and idols, all the abominations that were seen in the land of Judah and in Jerusalem, that he might perform the words of the law which were written in the book that Hilkiah the priest found in the house of the Lord* (2 Kings 23:24, emphasis added).

In Josiah's day (approx. 624 B.C.), "mediums and spiritists," "gods and idols," and numerous other "abominations" were being openly practiced among God's chosen people. Nearly a thousand years had passed since the time of Moses, and Israel was largely ignorant of what had been written in Leviticus and Deuteronomy. A reformation was needed.

What's this? a priest named Hilkiah wondered when he discovered old manuscripts hidden within the inner recesses of the Jewish temple. *A book containing the writings of Moses!* The manuscripts were quickly taken to the king. When Josiah read them, his eyes were opened. He saw exactly what God said about "familiar spirits" and other occult practices. Under deep conviction, and at the risk of being unpopular, Josiah boldly "put away those who consulted mediums and spiritists," and purged the land. This reformation was so remarkable that the Bible says there was "no king" like Josiah in Israel's entire history.

> *Now before him* [Josiah] *there was no king like him, who turned to the Lord with all his heart, with all his soul, and with all his might, according to all the Law of Moses; nor after him did any arise like him* (2 Kings 23:25).

A central part of Josiah's reformatory efforts was the removal of all "who consulted mediums and spiritists." I wish the producers of "Medium", "Ghost Whisperer", "Crossing Over With John Edward", and "The Lisa Williams Project" would read this. Perhaps they are honestly ignorant, just like King Josiah was before Hilkiah the priest showed him an ancient copy of the Book of the Law. Maybe Allison DuBois, James Van Praagh, John Edward, Carla Mae, Sylvia Browne, and other modern mediums are too. I don't know. I hope that is the case. It isn't my job to judge motives or decide destinies. I'm not qualified to issue such verdicts. Nevertheless, as a teacher of the Bible, I have a sacred responsibility to make God's Word plain. The solemn truth is that mediums, familiar spirits, and interaction with the dead are positively forbidden in the Holy Scriptures. "*Abomination*" is the word used.

To be fair, there is one Old Testament section about talking to the dead that has puzzled many, and a surface reading of the account has even led some to justify necromancy. (There's also one puzzling passage in the New

Testament, which we will examine later.) That *one*, unique Old Testament section describes a Jewish king named Saul who apparently talked to the ghost of the dead prophet Samuel. The story is found in First Samuel, chapter 28, verses 3-25. But as we shall plainly see—and as the esteemed Bible commentator Matthew Henry also affirms—Saul actually talked to a *demon in disguise*, not to Samuel. First we'll read the entire account. Then we shall look at the details.

Now Samuel had died, and all Israel had lamented for him and buried him in Ramah, in his own city. And Saul had put the mediums and the spiritists out of the land. Then the Philistines gathered together, and came and encamped at Shunem. So Saul gathered all Israel together, and they encamped at Gilboa. When Saul saw the army of the Philistines, he was afraid, and his heart trembled greatly. And when Saul inquired of the Lord, the Lord did not answer him, either by dreams or by Urim or by the prophets. Then Saul said to his servants, "Find me a woman who is a medium, that I may go to her and inquire of her." And his servants said to him, "In fact, there is a woman who is a medium at En Dor." So Saul disguised himself and put on other clothes, and he went, and two men with him; and they came to the woman by night. And he said, "Please conduct a séance for me, and bring up for me the one I shall name to you." Then the woman said to him, "Look, you know what Saul has done, how he has cut off the mediums and the spiritists from the land. Why then do you lay a snare for my life, to cause me to die?" And Saul swore to her by the Lord, saying, "As the Lord lives, no punishment shall come upon you for this thing." Then the woman said, "Whom shall I bring up for you?" And he said, "Bring up Samuel for me." When the woman saw Samuel, she cried out with a loud voice. And the woman spoke to Saul, saying, "Why have you deceived me? For you are Saul!" And the king said to her, "Do not be afraid. What did you see?" And the woman said to Saul, "I saw a spirit ascending out of the earth." So he said to her, "What is his form?" And she said, "An old man is coming up, and he is covered with a mantle." And Saul perceived that it was Samuel, and he stooped with his face to the ground and bowed down. Now Samuel said to Saul, "Why have you disturbed me by bringing me up?" And Saul answered, "I am deeply distressed; for the Philistines make war against me, and God has departed from me and does not answer me anymore, neither by prophets nor by dreams. Therefore I have called you, that you may reveal to me what I should do." Then Samuel said: "So why do you ask me, seeing the Lord has departed from you and has become your enemy? And the Lord has done for Himself as He spoke by me. For the Lord has torn the kingdom out of your hand and given it to your neighbor, David. Because you did not obey the voice of the Lord nor execute His fierce wrath upon Amalek, therefore the Lord has done this thing to you this day. Moreover the Lord will also deliver Israel with you into the hand of the Philistines. And tomorrow you and your sons will be with me. The Lord will also deliver the army of Israel into the hand of the Philistines." Immediately Saul fell full length on the ground, and was dreadfully afraid because of the words of Samuel. And there was no strength in him, for he had eaten no food all day or all night. And the woman came to Saul and saw that he was severely troubled, and said to him, "Look, your maidservant has obeyed your voice, and I have put my life in my hands and heeded the words which you spoke to me. Now therefore, please, heed also the voice of your maidservant, and let me set a piece of bread before you; and eat, that you may have strength when you go on your way." But he refused and said, "I will not eat." So his servants, together with the woman, urged him; and he heeded their voice. Then he arose from the ground and sat on the bed. Now the woman had a fatted calf in the house, and she hastened to kill it. And she took flour and kneaded it, and baked unleavened bread from it. So she brought it before Saul and his servants, and they ate. Then they rose and went away that night (1 Samuel 28:3-25).

Let's analyze this section, point by point. After the elderly prophet Samuel "had died," a vast Philistine army gathered together against King Saul and the Israelites. When Saul realized how ferocious the Philistine forces were, "he was afraid, and his heart trembled greatly." Nearing the end of his kingly career, this unfortunate leader had strayed far from his Creator. When the prophet Samuel was still alive, Saul had stubbornly ignored his instructions, and God's will (see 1 Sam. 15). The situation appeared ominous. Hoping against hope for heavenly help in an emergency, "Saul inquired of the Lord, [but] the Lord did not answer him, either by dreams or by Urim *or by the prophets.*" Note that last part. Whatever happened next, it wasn't *God* who was speaking to Saul, *nor one of His prophets.*

For many years King Saul had persistently rejected God's tender appeals, so the Lord decided that He would not now respond like a bus boy to Saul's emergency plea. In the Book of Proverbs, God makes His position plain:

Because I have called and you refused,
I have stretched out my hand and no one regarded,
Because you disdained all my counsel,
And would have none of my rebuke,
I also will laugh at your calamity;
I will mock when your terror comes,
When your terror comes like a storm,
And your destruction comes like a whirlwind,
When distress and anguish come upon you.
Then they will call on me, but I will not answer;
They will seek me diligently, but they will not find me
(Proverbs 1:24-28).

Unfortunately, this was Saul's plight. Heaven was silent. In this crisis hour, "Saul said to his servants, 'Find me a woman who is a medium, that I may go to her and inquire of her.' And his servants said to him, 'In fact, there is a woman who is a medium at En Dor.'" One of the most respected Bible commentators in Church history, Matthew Henry, comments:

> Saul seeks for a witch, v. 7. When God answered him not, if he
> had humbled himself by repentance and persevered in seeking God,
> who knows but that at length he might have been entreated for him?
> but, since he can discern no comfort either from heaven or earth (Isa.
> 8:21, 22), he resolves to knock at the gates of hell, and to see if any
> there will befriend him and give him advice: *Seek me a woman that
> has a familiar spirit*, v. 7.[5]

Saul knew exactly what Moses wrote in Deuteronomy 18, and by judicial authority he had even previously "put the mediums and the spiritists out of the land." But a few remained in hiding, and his servants remembered that there was a woman who practiced magic arts inside a cave at En Dor. So, taking two men with him, Saul disguised himself and "came to the woman by night."

What a scene is this! Israel's king, a man chosen to represent God on earth, disguises himself and, under cover of darkness, creeps like a lizard into a cave. Matthew Henry comments bluntly:

> Hearing of one [a medium] he hastens to her, but goes by night,
> and in disguise, only with two servants, and probably on foot, v. 8.
> See how those that are led captive by Satan are forced, 1. To disparage themselves. Never did Saul look so mean as when he went sneaking to a sorry witch to know his fortune. 2. To dissemble. Evil works
> are works of darkness, and they hate the light, neither care for coming to it. Saul went to the witch, not in his robes, but in the habit of
> a common soldier, not only lest the witch herself, if she had known
> him, should decline to serve him, either fearing he came to trepan
> her or resolving to be avenged on him for his edict against those of

her profession, but lest his own people should know it and abhor him for it. Such is the power of natural conscience that even those who do evil blush and are ashamed to do it.[6]

Upon finding the woman, Saul pleaded, "Please conduct a séance for me, and bring up for me the one I shall name to you." Take special note of this. Whoever or whatever is about to appear, it materialized at the command of a witch during a séance. This fact alone excludes the possibility that the ghost who showed up was the real prophet Samuel.

Hearing his request, the woman trembled. *Was this a trap?* She reminded this stranger (who was still unrecognized) of King Saul's own former edict against wizards and mediums. This must have stabbed the king's conscience. Here was a witch reminding him of his own law! The woman's comment, "Look, you know what *Saul has done*, how he has cut off the mediums and the spiritists of the land," teaches an important lesson. Matthew Henry wrote:

> Observe how sensible she is of danger from the edict of Saul, and what care she is in to guard against it; but not at all apprehensive of the obligations of God's law and the terrors of his wrath. She considered what *Saul* had done, not what God had done, against such practices, and feared a snare laid for her life more than a snare laid for her soul.[7]

How true this is! Some readers of *Demons in Disguise* may fault me for quoting Deuteronomy 18:11 and other Bible verses warning about mediums and spiritists. But instead of accusing me of judgmentalism or wrongdoing, they should ponder seriously that it is the great God of the Holy Bible who inspired these statements, not a mortal man. Our Creator is incredibly passionate about each one of us, and He sees secret snares laid for our souls. I don't wish to offend, but the truth must be told.

Seeking to alleviate her fears, Saul assured the woman that no harm would befall her. So, she prepared for her incantations, "Then the woman said, 'Whom shall I bring up for you?' And he said, 'Bring up Samuel for me.'" Again keep in mind that whoever or whatever is about to appear in the eerie illumination of flickering candlelight, it responded to the summons of a spiritualistic medium inside a dark mountain cave during a séance.

We don't know what spells or charms the witch used, but we do know that suddenly a ghostly apparition appeared, and that at the exact same moment the medium received the shock of her life. "And the woman spoke to Saul, saying, 'Why have you deceived me? For you are Saul!'" *How could she know this?* There is no hint in the text that she had visually penetrated the king's disguise. Matthew Henry insightfully commented:

> The witch, upon sight of the apparition, was aware that her client was Saul, *her familiar spirit, it is likely, informing her of it* (v. 12).[8]

Again Saul tried to calm her fears. "And the king said to her, 'Do not be afraid. *What did you see?*'" It's important to note that throughout this eerie encounter Saul himself never saw the spirit conjured by the medium. Only the woman did. The same thing often occurs when modern mediums give spiritual "readings" to their "clients," or visit haunted houses looking for ghosts. As the subtitle for the NBC "Medium" series declares, mediums "see what others can't." In *Visits From the Afterlife*, Sylvia Browne reports that often, even while the TV cameras are rolling, she alone suddenly perceives the presence of a ghost, while nobody else does. The crew may feel a creepy chill, yet they don't see anything beyond cameras and furniture. The same thing happened inside a dark cave before King Saul and his men.

"And the woman said to Saul, '*I saw* a spirit ascending out of the earth.'" Then Saul inquired, "What is his form?" This proves that Saul never saw the apparition; only the medium did. "And she said, 'An old man is coming up, and he is covered with a mantle.'" Now notice carefully the next sentence,

"*And Saul perceived that it was Samuel,* and he stooped with his face to the ground and bowed down." *Was it really Samuel?* Saul thought so, but does that make it so? We know his spiritual perceptions were quite dull at the time. Beyond this, think logically with me. Even if it *were* possible (more on this later) for the dead to talk to the living, would the spirit of the real prophet Samuel appear in a cave at the call of a medium? Hardly! Here's Matthew Henry's sober conclusion:

> God permitted the devil, to answer the design, to put on Samuel's shape, that those who would not *receive the love of the truth* might be *given up to strong delusions and believe a lie*...That the devil, by the divine permission, should be able to personate Samuel is not strange, since he can *transform himself into an angel of light!* nor is it strange that he should be permitted to do it upon this occasion, that Saul might be driven to despair, by enquiring of the devil, since he would not, in a right manner, enquire of the Lord, by which he might have had comfort.[9]

Mr. Henry's assessment fits the scriptural evidence. It was a *demon in disguise* that appeared to a witch in that cave. The entity then asked Saul, "Why have you disturbed me by bringing me up?" Saul replied by describing his dismal situation, the Philistine threat, and the Lord's refusal to answer him by dreams or prophets. "Therefore I have called you," Saul told the ghost, "that you may reveal to me what I should do." A dialog then occurs between the evil spirit and King Saul. Matthew Henry noted:

> We have here the conference between Saul and Satan. Saul came in disguise (v. 8), but Satan discovered him, v. 12. Satan comes in disguise, in the disguise of Samuel's mantle, and Saul cannot discover him. Such is the disadvantage we labour under, in wrestling with the *rulers of the darkness of this world*, that they know us, while we are ignorant of their wiles and devices.[10]

The apparition coldly replied, "So why do you ask me, seeing the Lord has departed from you and has become your enemy? And the Lord has done for Himself as He spoke by me. For the Lord has torn the kingdom out of your hand and given it to your neighbor, David. Because you did not obey the voice of the Lord nor execute His fierce wrath upon Amalek, therefore the Lord has done this thing to you this day."

This passage contains important lessons. The ghostly personage referred to specific past events and even quoted exact statements previously made by the prophet Samuel (when he was alive) about Saul's disobedience and about God's choice of someone else (a shepherd boy named David) to replace Saul as king of Israel. *This shows that demons have an intelligent awareness of specific events in people's past and that they will utilize this knowledge as part of their trickery.* Modern mediums—take heed! Just because an invisible entity knows intimate details about a deceased person, *this isn't proof that it is really that person.* It only proves that the particular spirit is smart—but not necessarily honest.

Impersonating Samuel, the lying spirit said, "The Lord...spoke by me," which implies that God was again speaking to Saul through His deceased prophet. But this is impossible, for the Bible specifically says that God was *no longer* speaking to Saul *by His prophets* (see 1 Sam. 28:6). Therefore this ghost was not Samuel the prophet. Here is Matthew Henry's analysis:

> Yet, to make him believe that he was Samuel, the apparition affirmed that it was God who spoke by him. The devil knows how to speak with an air of religion, and can teach *false apostles to transform themselves into the apostles of Christ* and imitate their language. Those who use spells and charms, and plead, in defense of them, that they find nothing in them but what is good, may remember what good words the devil here spoke, and yet with what a malicious design.[11]

"Moreover," the demon declared, "the Lord will also deliver Israel with you into the hand of the Philistines. And tomorrow you and your sons will be with me. The Lord will also deliver the army of Israel into the hand of the Philistines." This is precisely what happened (see 1 Sam. 31). Thus demons can—in a limited sense—sometimes foretell the future. Those who trust fortune tellers should be aware of this. Just because a person, or a spirit, accurately predicts some pending event, this is no proof of divine inspiration.

Even though his brain is in a fallen condition, the devil is far from stupid. He's been around for a long time, is a keen observer, and can even make certain events occur to fulfill his "predictions." In the case of Saul, satan knew God had departed from Him, had withdrawn His protection, and that he had him under his power.

"Immediately Saul fell full length on the ground, and was dreadfully afraid because of the words of Samuel. And there was no strength in him, for he had eaten no food all day or all night." Earlier in this dark dialog Saul had asked the entity whom he "perceived" to be Samuel what he should do; but now he received no such guidance—only a dire prediction of approaching doom for himself and his sons. This counsel snuffed out Saul's last flicker of hope. Mr. Henry observed:

> Satan had helped him to palliate and excuse that sin when Samuel was dealing with him to bring him to repentance, but now he aggravates it, to make him despair of God's mercy. See what those get that hearken to Satan's temptations. He himself will be their accuser, and insult over them.[12]

The doomed king staggered to his feet, ate some food, "Then they rose and went away that night." Just 24 hours later, King Saul and his sons were dead. First his sons were slain in battle. As the Philistines advanced for the kill, Saul realized all was lost, so he committed suicide to avoid being captured and tortured. "So Saul, his three sons, his armorbearer, and all his men died together that same day together" (1 Sam. 31:6). The Bible reports:

*So Saul died for his unfaithfulness which he had committed against the Lord, because he did not keep the word of the Lord, **and also because he consulted a medium for guidance*** (1 Chronicles 10:13, emphasis added).

Such was the bitter end of a man who rejected God's counsel and sought assistance from a ghost in a cave. Echoing down the corridors of time, this message from the ancient prophet Isaiah speaks to our generation:

*And when they say to you, "Seek those who are mediums and wizards, who whisper and mutter," should not a people seek their God? **Should they seek the dead** on behalf of the living? To the law and to the testimony! If they do not speak according to this word, it is because there is no light in them* (Isaiah 8:19-20, emphasis added).

Isaiah said we must choose who we will "seek." The options are plain. We can either seek the living God, or *"seek the dead."* We can trust familiar spirits who "whisper and mutter," or the "word" of our loving Creator. Isaiah also testified that every doctrine or teaching should be carefully compared with "the law" (the writings of Moses) and "the testimony" of God's prophets. This is how we can test their validity. If professional mediums, apparitions, or invisible personalities don't agree with God's Book, "it is because there is no light in them."

Bible truth is our safeguard against invisible personalities who may seem friendly, but whose secret agenda is either to push human beings toward their death (as with King Saul), or to turn them into lunatics who inhabit cemeteries (remember Mark, chapter 5). On the other hand, satan seems content to allow professional mediums to keep their sanity for a while (as with the witch in the cave) and even to prosper financially. But it's all a trick. He's just biding his time, becoming more sure of his victims. Mark my words: someday he will reveal his true colors.

I will close this chapter with something amazing. If you log onto the Internet and find Merriam-Webster's Online Dictionary, try typing the words "familiar spirit" into the search field, and see what you find. I just did it. These words popped up, "One entry found for familiar spirit." Two definitions are listed. The second one reads:

2: the spirit of a dead person invoked by a medium to advise or prophesy.

There's no controversy about this part. Modern mediums believe this to be true, and Hollywood producers are profiting on the acute public interest in dead people. But it's the first definition that is the most surprising. When I first saw it, I could hardly believe my eyes. Even Merriam-Webster's Dictionary tells the truth! Take a look. The primary definition of "familiar spirit" is this:

1. a spirit or demon that serves or prompts an individual.[13]

This is my point exactly.

ENDNOTES

1. See http://www.m-w.com/dictionary/necromancy.

2. See http://www.online-bibleconcordance.com/Dictionary.aspx.

3. Allison DuBois, *Don't Kiss Them Goodbye* (New York: Simon and Shuster, 2004), 176, emphasis added.

4. Sylvia Browne, *Visits From the Afterlife* (London: New American Library, a division of Penguin books, 2003), 43, emphasis added.

5. Matthew Henry's Bible Commentary (online edition), see http://blueletterbible.org/Comm/mhc/1Sa/1Sa028.html).

6. Ibid.

7. Ibid.

8. Ibid, emphasis added.

9. Ibid.

10. Ibid.

11. Ibid.

12. Ibid.

13. See http://www.m-w.com/dictionary/familiar%20spirit, emphasis added.

Chapter 8

THE TRAIL
OF THE SERPENT

The farther backward you can look, the farther forward you are likely to see.

—Winston Churchill (1874-1965),
British Prime Minister, Orator, Writer

"IN the beginning God created the heavens and the earth" (Gen. 1:1). This sublime statement is the first sentence found in the first book of the Bible. It is simple, yet profound, and reveals the biblical position that planet Earth did not evolve over billions of years, but was supernaturally "created" by an almighty Designer—the Maker of Heaven and earth. The Bible doesn't support "The Big Bang Theory," unless it is interpreted to mean, "God spoke, and bang!"

Believe it or not, the best way to comprehend the mysteries of life, death, evil, and even the issue of talking to dead people, is to go back to the dawn of time by studying the Book of Genesis. Genesis chapter 1 reveals that a magnificent Maker created planet Earth, the atmosphere, and our entire solar system in one literal week. God made the light (first day), the sky (second day), the earth (third day), the sun, moon, and stars (fourth day), birds and fish (fifth day), animals and crawling creatures, and then finally, "man" in His own image (sixth day). Genesis chapter 2 caps it all off by declaring:

And on the seventh day God ended His work which He had done, and He rested on the seventh day from all His work which He had done (Genesis 2:2).

Thus God made the world in six literal, 24-hour days, and rested on the seventh day. This simple yet profound fact explains why there are seven days in the week and is an important testimony to the truthfulness of God's Book. Genesis chapter 2 zooms in more specifically on the creation of man and adds this personal touch:

And the Lord God formed man of the dust of the ground, and breathed into his nostrils the breath of life; and man became a living soul (Genesis 2:7).

Here is the truth of man's origin and composition. We didn't evolve from cosmic soup, goop, slime, or monkeys, but the first man was "formed" by a divine touch from a Master's hand. Exquisite eyes, functioning brain, beating heart, the ability to hear, speak, and love—this is all the work of God. The truth is that human beings are miraculous from head to toe. "Natural Selection" can't be held responsible for such complexity. It is a physiological impossibility.

After breathing "the breath of life" into man, the first created human *"became a living soul."* This is important. The biblical formula is: dust + breath = a living soul. "A living soul" is what man is, essentially. God called the first living soul "Adam." Later in Genesis chapter 2, He created Eve (see Gen. 2:20-

24). "The Lord God planted a garden eastward in Eden, and there He put the man whom He had formed" (Gen. 2:8). Adam and Eve's original home was not an apartment located on a downtown street corner inside a smoggy city, but a lush garden filled with fragrant plants, exotic birds, colorful flowers, and delicious fruit. It was a perfect Paradise.

The God of the Bible is not only remarkably creative and highly personal, but also supremely loving. "God is love" (1 John 4:8), the New Testament informs us. Love is the actuating force, the primary motive, and the guiding principle behind everything God says and does. It even motivates His warnings; and this is especially true of the first warning ever given to the human family:

And the Lord God commanded the man, saying, "Of every tree of the garden you may freely eat; but of the tree of the knowledge of good and evil you shall not eat, for in the day that you eat of it you shall surely die" (Genesis 2:16-17).

"God is love." Love, by its very nature, involves freedom; and freedom, by its very nature, involves choice. There is no love without freedom to choose either to love or not to love. Love and freedom are flip sides of the same coin and are the two principles that God values most (and as we will soon see, He is willing to die for them). And if you think about it, we value them too. I love my wife Kristin and our little boy, Seth; and of course, I want them to love me. There would be nothing satisfying about Kristin mechanically repeating, "Steve, I love you," or Seth stoically saying, "I love you, Daddy," if they were forced to do so. It is the *freedom* to love, and the *choice* to love, that make life worth living.

True love also implies loyalty, and loyalty implies obedience to right principles, especially when our loyalty is tested. On April 9, 2000, I stood before relatives, guests, my bride-to-be dressed in white, and God Himself. I was then asked by a minister, "Do you, Steve Wohlberg, take this woman to be your lawfully wedded wife? Will you love her, support her, cherish her, and forsaking all others, cleave to her, for better or for worse, in sickness and in health, until death do you part?" "I do," was my heartfelt reply. As I write this, Kristin and I have been married for almost seven wonderful years. Our marriage—and every marriage—will stand or fall based on our continual choices to love each other, to remain loyal to each other, to obey right principles, and to *forsake all others* when tempted to violate our vows.

In the Garden of Eden, eating or not eating from "the tree of the knowledge of good and evil" was God's test. To this one restriction, obedience was required. Motivated by love and infinite wisdom, God gave Adam and Eve the opportunity to demonstrate their love and loyalty to Him by obeying what He said. "Don't eat from that tree!" was His direct command. And what made this test so real was the existence of a tempter. Remember, the Book of Revelation says that after the devil was booted out of Heaven, "he was cast to *the earth*, and his angels were cast out with him" (Rev. 12:9). Satan was allowed access to that one tree.

God warned Adam, His newly created "living soul," that if he ate from that one forbidden tree, the consequences would be disastrous. "*You shall surely die,*" the Lord emphatically declared. This was the first warning given in the Bible. Shortly thereafter, in Genesis chapter 3, the drama began, and as we are about to discover, this vital chapter is not only filled with practical lessons for every human being on planet Earth today, but it contains vital information about life, death, and talking to dead people.

Now the serpent was more cunning than any beast of the field which the Lord God had made. And he said to the woman, "Has God indeed said, 'You shall not eat of every tree of the garden'?" And the woman said to the serpent, "We may eat the fruit of the trees of the garden; but of the fruit of the tree which is in the midst of the garden, God has said, 'You shall not eat it, nor shall you touch it, lest you die.'" Then the serpent said to the woman, "You will not surely die. For God knows that in the day you eat of it your eyes will be opened, and you will be like God, knowing good and evil" (Genesis 3:1-5).

The "serpent" itself was a creature "which the Lord God had made." But God hadn't given animals the ability to talk, so the mere fact that this reptile began speaking to Eve demonstrates that there was a separate intelligence operating through the mind of the snake. So when the Bible states, "... *the serpent said* to the woman" (verse 4), it wasn't actually the physical serpent that was talking, but someone else who was speaking through its reptilian lips. That serpent was the first medium in human history.

Lucifer, talking through the snake, said to Eve, "Has God indeed said, 'You shall not eat of every tree of the garden'?" His first words were designed to instill doubt about what "God indeed said." From the start, his reasoning was twisted. God had indeed given to Adam and Eve the freedom to eat from "every tree of the garden," except that one tree. And His restriction was entirely reasonable. But the serpent's question raised subtle suspicion about God's integrity, fairness, and truthfulness.

"And the woman said to the serpent..." This was Eve's first mistake; she should never have dialoged with this creature in the first place. No doubt God had told her about the existence of a fallen foe, and His warning about not eating from that one tree should have been enough to keep her away, not only from the tree itself, but also from any stranger who might wish to converse about it. But because she didn't *see* any evil personality lurking nearby, and because *the voice* she heard undoubtedly *sounded* pleasant, she was caught off guard and enticed. Again, modern mediums should take heed. Things are not always what they appear to be.

Eve replied that she and her husband were indeed free to eat from every tree in the garden, except the forbidden one. About that one tree alone, Eve reported, "God has said, 'You shall not eat it, nor shall you touch it, lest you die.'" Thus Eve repeated God's words to the snake. Now notice carefully the serpent's response:

> Then the serpent said to the woman, "**You will not surely die**. For God knows that in the day you eat of it your eyes will be opened, and you will be like God, knowing good and evil" (Genesis 3:4-5, emphasis added).

This single sentence should be placed under a spiritual microscope. Because so much is at stake here, I'm going to isolate five points that arise from the text, one by one, so you won't miss them. Let these five points sink deeply into your heart:

1. "You will not surely die" is *the first lie* recorded in the Holy Bible.

2. "You will not surely die" is *the first lie* told to a human being.

3. "You will not surely die" is a direct challenge to God and His Word.

4. "You will not surely die" was spoken by the serpent.

5. "You will not surely die" is *a lie*.

"You will *surely* die," God warned. "You will *not* surely die," countered the snake. Who told the truth, God or satan? The question resounds to our day. The serpent continued, "For God knows that in the day you eat of it your eyes will be opened, and you will be like God, knowing good and evil" (Gen. 3:5). "Don't be silly!" the serpent basically said, "There's no death penalty for sin. Instead, life and happiness await you. Your eyes will be opened," he whispered slyly, "and you will be like God, knowing good and evil." Enlightenment, god-hood, and *no death*—these were the promises made by the snake.

Eve pondered lucifer's temptation as heavenly beings watched intently. Holy angels and fallen legions held their breath. God Himself probably sat at the edge of His throne. Two conflicting voices now rattled inside Eve's pretty head: "You will surely die" or "You will not surely die." Both ideas clashed within her brain. What should she do? The results of her choice would ripple far beyond her limited comprehension. Tragically:

So when the woman saw that the tree was good for food, that it was pleasant to the eyes, and a tree desirable to make one wise, she took of its fruit and ate (Genesis 3:6).

After dialoging with the snake, Eve suddenly "saw" that the tree was "good for food." Her perception had become warped, as was Saul's when he "perceived" a deadly demon to be the deceased prophet Samuel. Of course, the forbidden tree was "pleasant to the eyes," but we should never trust what our "eyes" see above what God says. Eve also perceived the tree to be "desirable to make one wise"—what a complete illusion! The devil's wisdom is infernal. True wisdom comes from God alone and is manifested by obedience to His Word. Fully duped by a cunning devil, Eve stretched out her hand, "took of its fruit and ate."

We don't know exactly what Eve said to her husband, but no doubt she urged him to take a bite. "She also gave to her husband with her," the text informs us (Gen. 3:6). "Try it, Sweetie," she might have said excitedly. Earlier in Genesis 3, a beady-eyed reptile had become the channel for satan's mind. Now who was the unconscious conduit for that same deceptive entity? Why, it was Adam's beautiful wife, Eve! Do you think she was aware of this? Hardly! This should impress us that wicked spirits can easily operate through unsuspecting people without their realizing it. Again, modern mediums, beware.

Who knows how long Adam wrestled with his heart-wrenching choice. *Eve or God, Eve or God?* he must have pondered. There Eve stood, as beautiful as ever. *Maybe the serpent was right?* Although his conscience was probably screaming, "Don't do it!" Adam finally decided to brave the consequences. He loved Eve; and he would share her fate. The Bible simply

says, "and he ate." Three little words. One tiny act. The results would rever-
berate to the close of time.

Then the eyes of both of them were opened, and they knew that they were
naked; and they sewed fig leaves together and made themselves coverings
(Genesis 3:7).

"Your eyes will be opened," the devil said. In a twisted sense, he was right.
The eyes of Adam and Eve were opened on that fateful day, but what they saw
next wasn't what they expected. Instead of profound spiritual enlightenment,
"they knew that they were naked." A sudden chill crept over their bare bodies
that paralleled a cold sense of guilt that invaded their souls. Horror took hold
of them, and they were absolutely terrified! *What have we done? We have*
betrayed our Maker! What will happen next? Fearful of appearing before a
Holy God in their sinful state, "they sewed fig leaves together and made themselves coverings."

And they heard the sound of the Lord God walking in the garden in the
cool of the day, and Adam and his wife hid themselves from the presence
of the Lord God among the trees of the garden. Then the Lord God
called to Adam and said to him, "Where are you?" So he said, "I heard
Your voice in the garden, and I was afraid because I was naked; and I
hid myself." And He said, "Who told you that you were naked? Have you
eaten from the tree of which I commanded you that you should not eat?"
(Genesis 3:8-11).

What a tragic day! Instead of welcoming their Maker, Adam and Eve "hid
themselves from the presence of the Lord God among the trees of the garden."
That's what sin does. It leads sinners to hide amid shadows, fearful of the light.
When God inquired of Adam, "Where are you?" He knew his whereabouts,
but He wanted to give Adam an opportunity to explain himself, plus He
wanted his response to be a lesson for all generations—for you and me.

"Have you eaten from the tree of which I commanded you that you should not eat?" the Lord asked. This was a simple, straightforward question, which should have been met by a simple, straightforward response. Adam should have hung his head and honestly replied, "Yes, I did." But because he had sinned, his mind had now become infected with a new spirit of self-justification. A simple answer was not so easy. Notice carefully the evasive response of both Adam and Eve to God's direct inquiry:

*Then the man said, "The **woman** whom **You** gave to be with me, she gave me of the tree, and I ate." And the Lord God said to the woman, "What is this that you have done?" The woman said, "The **serpent** deceived me, and I ate"* (Genesis 3:12-13, emphasis added).

Both Adam and Eve finally admitted, "I ate," but their guilty admissions were tacked onto the very last part of their confessions. First, Adam blamed Eve, and then he even blamed God for making her. Eve blamed the serpent before she acknowledged any mistake on her part. One big lesson is: It is difficult for guilty souls to admit their guilt. It's much easier to blame, to justify, and to find excuses. Another lesson is: If we are ever to get back to the garden, the place to start is by being honest, by humbling ourselves, and by candidly acknowledging our sins. This can only be done by the grace of God and by fully accepting His Word.

The Lord then cursed the serpent (verse 14), promised hope for fallen humanity (verse 15), declared that women would suffer during childbirth (verse 16), and cursed the earth so that it would bear thorns and thistles (verses 17 and 18). Now notice carefully God's last recorded words spoken directly to Adam at the close of this momentous dialog,

*In the sweat of your face you shall eat bread, **till you return to the ground**. For out of it were you taken; **for dust you are, and to dust you shall return*** (Genesis 3:19, emphasis added).

In this final sentence, God defined the consequences of sin. Adam, Eve, and their descendants would "return to the ground." "For dust you are," God sadly informed Adam, "and to dust you shall return." Have you ever heard the phrase, "Ashes to ashes, dust to dust"? Ministers at funerals often speak it. Now you know where it came from. It was the Creator Himself who declared that because man was taken *out of* the ground, he would *return* to the ground. Because of sin, man's immediate destiny is "dust." The lyrics of a 1970s rock 'n' roll song, "Dust in the Wind," repeat this truth. "Dust in the wind," the lead singer of Kansas still sings, "All we are is dust in the wind." The wind blows, the dust scatters, then it disappears.

The last three verses of Genesis chapter 3 are rarely quoted in sermons, or explained in religious books; in fact, they usually remain unnoticed, even by biblical scholars. Yet they contain truths so significant that they should be emblazoned on skyscrapers. Genesis 3—the only chapter in the Bible that describes in detail the fall of man—concludes with this amazing, inspired information:

> *Then the Lord God said, "Behold, the man has become like one of Us, to know good and evil.* ***And now, lest he put out his hand and take also from the tree of life, and eat, and live forever****—therefore the Lord God sent him out of the garden of Eden to till the ground from which he was taken. So He drove out the man; and He placed Cherubim at the east of the garden of Eden, and a flaming sword which turned every way,* ***to guard the way to the tree of life*** *(Genesis 3:22-24, emphasis added).*

The forbidden tree—"the tree of the knowledge of good and evil"—was not the only special tree that God planted in the midst of Paradise. "*The tree of life was also in the midst of the garden*" (Gen. 2:9). "The tree of life" was another unique tree. According to the text, its fruit would enable its eater to "live forever." In other words, it perpetuated immortality. God created Adam as a "living soul" (Gen. 2:7), but then He warned that if he ate from the forbidden tree, he would "surely die" (Gen. 2:17). But because of the serpent's subtlety, both Adam and Eve swallowed that deadly fruit. And now, as a result of their inexcusable disobedience, they were sinners awaiting the death sentence.

According to Genesis 3:22, God pondered this awful reality. For the good of the entire universe for ceaseless ages, Supreme Rulers made a key decision on their throne. They decided that fallen man *must not* be allowed to "put out his hand and take also from the tree of life, and eat, and live forever." Consider this closely. Again, according to the text, God did not want Adam and Eve, *in their sinful state*, to "live forever." If they did, this would mean two things:

1. God's Word, "*You will surely die*," would be nullified.

2. Sin itself would exist forever.

To prevent these unthinkable abnormalities, Genesis 3:22-24 says that God initiated four distinct measures to prevent Adam and Eve from partaking of "the tree of life":

(1) **Banishment:** "Therefore the Lord God sent him out of the garden of Eden to till the ground from which he was taken." Adam and Eve were banished from Paradise (where "the tree of life" had been planted) and forced to make their home elsewhere on the earth.

(2) **Cherubim Guardians:** "He placed Cherubim at the east of the garden of Eden." The choice of "Cherubim" as guardians of the gate is significant. As we saw earlier, lucifer was originally "an anointed cherub" before God's throne (see Ezek. 28:14). For God to pick Cherubim (two "cherubs") for this important task reveals that He was now appointing two of lucifer's former counterparts to counteract the devil's own work.

(3) **Flaming Swords:** God provided His mighty Cherubim ambassadors with "a flaming sword that turned every way." These shiny blades were more lethal than any fictitious light saber

portrayed in any George Lucas *Star Wars* flick. They blazed constantly.

(4) **Specific Assignment:** God's sword-wielding Cherubim were assigned one all-important task: "*to guard the way to the tree of life.*" The tree of life—whose fruit perpetuated immortality—must be kept from the reach of sentenced-to-death sinners at all costs.

We can be certain that neither Adam, nor Eve, nor any of their fallen descendants ever passed through that superhuman guard. It's true that God did give Adam and Eve a choice about whether "to eat or not to eat" from the first tree, "the tree of the knowledge of good and evil." But concerning the second tree, "the tree of life," no such choice was given. Overwhelming force was used.

The core message of Genesis 3:22-24 is that no sinner has ever eaten from "the tree of life," *therefore sinners do not naturally "live forever."* That's what the text says. Because Adam and Eve obeyed the snake and sank their teeth into forbidden fruit, fallen human beings are now mortal, not immortal. Notice how Merriam-Webster's Online Dictionary defines "mortal," "immortal," and "immortality":

Mortal
Function: adjective
2a: subject to death [1]

Immortal
Function: adjective
1a: exempt from death [2]

Immortality
Function: adjective
1a: unending existence [3]

These same exact words are in the Holy Bible. Now look at what God's Word says about each term, and especially to whom each is applied:

*Shall **mortal man** be more just than God? Shall a man be more pure than his maker?* (Job 4:17 KJV, emphasis added).

[Fallen man] *exchanged the glory of the **immortal God** for images made to look like **mortal man** and birds and animals and reptiles* (Romans 1:23, emphasis added).

*Now to the King eternal, **immortal**, invisible, the only God, be honor and glory for ever and ever. Amen* (1 Timothy 1:17, emphasis added).

[God] ***only hath immortality**, dwelling in the light which no man can approach unto; whom no man has seen, nor can see: to whom be honour and power everlasting. Amen* (1 Timothy 6:16 KJV, emphasis added).

These verses are exceedingly clear. Fallen man is now "mortal," or subject to death, whereas God "only hath immortality," or unending existence. Now let's put some pieces together. The activity of mediums, spiritists, and spiritualists (in both ancient and modern times) is entirely based upon the belief that it is now possible to talk to dead people. Everyone knows this. But think about it. What is this belief based upon? Here's the kicker. This belief is entirely rooted in the prior idea that human beings today are *naturally immortal*, that we *naturally* "live forever," that there is *no death*, and therefore, that *the dead aren't really dead*. This is as true as the fact that a Rabbi is Jewish.

Here's the proof. March 31, 1848, is considered the official birth date of Modern Spiritualism. On that notable night in 1848, inside the famous Hydesville Cottage in upper New York State, ten-year-old Margaret Fox and her nine-year-old sister Kate were suddenly awakened from their slumbers by loud pounding on the walls of their bedroom. During the previous month they had witnessed similar noises, including window-rattling and heavy thuds down the pantry stairs; but on this particular night the pounding was louder than normal.

The girls sprang from the beds. "Mr. Splitfoot, do as I do," Kate instructed the ghost with childlike simplicity. She clapped her hands. The same number of raps followed instantly. Moments later, Margaret held up five fingers. Five more raps quickly followed. "Look, Mama," Katie explained, "it can see as well as hear!" Their otherworldly guest soon identified itself as the spirit of a murdered peddler by the name of Charles B. Rosna, whose corpse—the ghost explained—lay buried in the cellar of their home. Years later, skeletal remains were discovered hidden behind a basement wall in that very house.

The night of March 31, 1848, was just the beginning. The mysterious New York "rappings" continued, the Fox sisters soon became famous, Modern Spiritualism was born, and its beliefs spread like a forest fire around the world. Apparently, the spirit world had crossed the veil, and now life-after-death communication was confirmed. Even today, the names "Kate and Margaret Fox" are still spoken reverently by spiritualists, and the New York site of the original house attracts thousands of visitors. The Hydesville Memorial Park remains as a witness. A monument has been erected, bearing this inscription:

ERECTED DECEMBER 4, 1927
BY THE
SPIRITUALISTS OF THE WORLD
IN COMMEMORATION OF THE
ADVENT OF
MODERN SPIRITUALISM
AT HYDESVILLE, N.Y., MARCH 31, 1848
AND IN TRIBUTE TO SPIRITUALISM, THE ROCK
UPON WHICH DEMONSTRABLE SPIRITUALISM
FOREVER STANDS
THERE IS NO DEATH
THERE ARE NO DEAD [4]

"*There is no death; there are no dead.*" Based on their memorialized testimony, this is "the rock" upon which "spiritualism forever stands." The idea is not new. Amazingly, a snake in Paradise who slyly whispered to a perfect woman, "You will not surely die" was the first to speak it. Eve should have known better, but she was caught in a trap. Sadly, she wasn't the only one.

Two Cherubim with fiery swords reveal the truth.

ENDNOTES

1. See http://www.m-w.com/dictionary/mortal.

2. See http://www.m-w.com/dictionary/Immortal.

3. See http://www.m-w.com/dictionary/Immortality.

4. See http://www.angelfire.com/nj/writeups/Hydesville.html, emphasis added.

Chapter 9

THE RESURRECTION FACTOR

Christ the Lord is risen today, Al–le–lu–ia!
Sons of men and angels say, Al–le–lu–ia!
Death in vain forbids Him rise, Al–le–lu–ia!
Christ has opened Paradise, Al–le–lu–ia!

—Charles Wesley,
English hymn writer, poet, preacher (1707-1788)
Taken from his classic hymn, "Christ the Lord Is Risen Today"

ADAM and Eve could scarcely believe what they had just heard. "For dust you are," God had uncompromisingly announced, "and to dust you shall return" (Gen. 3:19). How long had they been alive so far? No one knows for sure. But we can be certain that the thought of dying terrified them both. *Dust! Aghh! Why did we listen to that snake!* Adam probably reproached Eve bitterly. What would happen next?

We've already read Genesis 3:22-24, which describes Adam and Eve's eviction from Paradise, the Cherubim sentinels with fiery swords, and the guarding of the tree of the life, yet sandwiched between verse 19 (the "dust" sentence) and verses 22-24 (the Cherubim section) are two little verses, one of which contains the first unveiling of an eternal secret:

And Adam called his wife's name Eve; because she was the mother of all living. Unto Adam also and to his wife did the Lord God make **coats of skins, and clothed them** *(Genesis 3:20-21, emphasis added).*

Shortly after their sin, Adam and Eve "sewed fig leaves together and made themselves coverings" (Gen. 3:7). Those fig leaves represented their flimsy attempt to cover their sin. On a much larger spiritual scale, fig leaves represent the ongoing efforts of fallen human beings throughout history—up to this very day—to cover themselves with their own righteousness and to save themselves by their own works. Genesis 3:21 reveals how utterly worthlessness such efforts are. Plant leaves won't cut it. Instead, "the Lord God made coats of skins, and clothed them."

Those "coats of skins" came from animals. Obviously, the only way animal skins could become garments for Adam and Eve would be if one or more animals were put to death. Now keep in mind, at this point in time, "death" itself was unknown throughout the entire universe. Nothing—absolutely nothing—had *ever* died. Adam and Eve hardly knew what "death" meant. Yes, God had warned, "You will surely die," but this fearful statement was dimly comprehended. This was about to change. Imagine the following scene:

"Adam," God may have said, "Do you see that lamb underneath that fig tree? Yes, that one, the one snuggling up to its mother. Go pick it up and bring it here." This time Adam obeyed instantly, while Eve watched nervously. Standing before his Maker with a trusting lamb in his arms, God may have handed Adam a sharp object; or perhaps Adam was instructed to make a sharp object first. "Baa..." said the lamb softly, without a trace of fear.

"Now hold it firmly with your left arm close to your chest, and hold this knife tightly in your right hand." Adam's heart began beating wildly. Glancing down at the unsuspecting animal, their eyes met. Even today, animal eyes often reveal unusual depth and intelligence. "Adam gave names to all cattle, to the birds of the air, and to every beast of the field" (Gen. 2:20) before he had eaten the forbidden fruit. He would have named that lamb, too.

The silence was deafening. Adam, Eve, loyal angels, legions of dark forces, and lucifer himself all stood breathlessly, momentarily frozen in time, perched on the edge of an event that was previously unimaginable. For the first time ever, an intelligent life was about to end. It wouldn't be an accident, but a calculated, deliberate sacrifice. Suddenly the lamb tensed, sensing unexpected danger. "Now!" God commanded firmly, shattering the silence. *"Do it now!"* Taking a deep breath, Adam obediently plunged the sharp object deep into the furry body cradled in his arms.

The creature yelped in pain. Eve screamed. Then to Adam's utter horror, bright red fluid splattered onto his face, hands, arms, and chest. Adam dropped the lamb, which fell at his feet, convulsing violently. It was a moment of bizarre camaraderie as all eyes—good and evil alike—were corporately glued to the unfortunate creature as it coughed, writhed, jerked, and groaned on the ground. Finally, the animal stopped moving entirely. No breath. No sound. No movement. Nothing. Open eyes stared vacantly into space. There was silence again. The horrific tragedy rippled beyond the stars. *The animal was dead.*

The first two stanzas of a song written by Vince Christian entitled, "The Caretakers," tells the story:

The Caretakers are gone, There is an aching loneliness.
No one but God can see, what is to come.
Adam cradles the lamb to his chest, as the universe collectively recoils.

The warm red blood soaks into the wool.
And spatters on the altar rocks.

Many nights he woke in sweat, remembering the lamb
That he had named. Kicking, bleating, going limp,
With eyes so trusting to the end.
He wants to spit the apple out, and he cries out to Eve,
"What have we done, what have we done?" [1]

So this is what death means! Adam and Eve must have concluded together. *How awful!* At that moment, God's previous warning, "You will surely die," took on new meaning. It was one thing to *hear* their Maker warn about the death sentence, but it was another thing entirely to watch death suck out the life of its first victim. *We caused this!* the fallen couple realized bitterly.

As Adam and Eve watched that first lamb die, another question may have rattled their guilty consciences. *Why the lamb?* Hadn't God said that *they* would "surely die"? Why did an innocent furry creature have to be sacrificed? If they did ponder this question, surely God discerned their unspoken thought. He also understood the cosmic consequences of their small act of blatant disobedience—consequences that are impossible for human beings to fully grasp. The truth is that when Adam's knife first pierced that innocent furry body, an infinitely deeper pain immediately penetrated God's heart. We'll never fully understand it. Angels bow their knees as they ponder it. The prince of darkness remains baffled by it.

O My Son! a Father realized. *O My Father!* His Son replied. That first bleeding lamb! O the depth of its hidden message! Unknown to Adam and Eve, that innocent animal symbolized the sacrifice of One later referred to as "the Lamb slain from the foundation of the world" (Rev. 13:8). Why wasn't the death penalty immediately executed upon Adam and Eve the moment they sinned? *Because a ransom had been found.*

We don't know how many innocent animals had to be sacrificed in order for Adam and Eve to have a new set of clothes to replace their plant leaves. But eventually, the garments were ready, and "the Lord God made coats of skins, and clothed them" (Gen. 3:21). An eternal truth lies hidden within this solitary passage. Again, God told Adam that he would "surely die" if he sinned. After the first man disobeyed, an invincible pair of Cherubim with flashing swords barred access to "the tree of life" so that no sinner might naturally "live forever" in a fallen state. The situation was frightening and dismal. Then an animal was slain, which prophetically pointed forward to a greater sacrifice to come, offering hope that all was not lost. "Eternal life" remained a possibility, but it could come from *only one source.* The following verses clearly show who that source is:

*For God so loved the world that He gave His only begotten Son, that whoever **believes in Him** should not perish but have **eternal life*** (John 3:16, emphasis added).

*And this is the testimony: that God has given to us **eternal life**, and **this life is in His Son**. He who has the Son has life: but he who does not have the Son of God does not have life* (1 John 5:11-12, emphasis added).

*For the wages of sin is death, but the gift of God is **eternal life in Christ Jesus our Lord*** (Romans 6:23, emphasis added).

These Bible passages plainly teach that although, because of sin, fallen man doesn't naturally "live forever" (Gen. 3:24), "eternal life" has nevertheless become accessible through *Jesus Christ alone.* "Eternal life," John testified, "is in His Son." Through symbolism, this merciful truth was revealed to Adam and Eve shortly after they ate the forbidden fruit. Animal skins that represented the spotless righteousness of a future Savior who would be fully able to cover sin proclaimed it. But here's the catch. In the Book of Genesis, before

God could place those skins upon Adam and Eve, the animals had to die. The Bible's unfathomable message is that the same thing had to happen to God's own Son. Like an innocent lamb in His Father's arms, Jesus must be sacrificed in behalf of sinners. This is the mystery of redemption. There was no other way. Sin—because of its ugly nature—merits the death penalty. In order for the Maker of Heaven and earth to maintain the integrity of His Word and divine government, that death sentence must be carried out.

Fast-forward approximately 4,000 years later to a lonely hill outside the city of Jerusalem. "Eli, Eli, lama sabachthani!" (Matt. 26:46) cries the Innocent One as He hangs upon a cross. The death of the first animal in Eden foreshadowed this exact moment. Its message was repeated when Abel—the second son of Adam and Eve—roped a lamb to an altar just beyond the gates of Paradise (see Gen. 4:4). It was reiterated by the sacrifices of Noah (see Gen. 8:20) Abraham (see Gen. 22:13), and other ancient patriarchs. It was hidden within the Passover blood that the Israelites dripped on their doorposts on the night of their deliverance from Egyptian slavery (see Exod. 12:23). For over a thousand years, it was proclaimed every time a lamb, dove, goat, bull, or ram was slain in the courts of the Jewish Temple (see Lev. 4). This entire bloody history pointed forward to the death of one Divine Person. The prophet Isaiah predicted it when he wrote:

Who has believed our report?
And to whom has the arm of the Lord been revealed?
For He shall grow up before Him as a tender plant,
And as a root out of dry ground.
He has no form or comeliness;
And when we see Him,
There is no beauty that we should desire Him.
He is despised and rejected by men,
A Man of sorrows and acquainted with grief.
And we hid, as it were, our faces from Him;

He was despised, and we did not esteem Him.

Surely He has borne our griefs and carried our sorrows;

Yet we esteemed Him stricken,

Smitten by God, and afflicted.

But He was wounded for our transgressions,

He was bruised for our iniquities;

The chastisement for our peace was upon Him,

And by His stripes we are healed.

All we like sheep have gone astray;

We have turned, every one, to his own way;

And the Lord has laid on Him the iniquity of us all.

He was oppressed and He was afflicted,

Yet He opened not His mouth;

He was led as a lamb to the slaughter,

And as a sheep before its shearers is silent,

So He opened not His mouth (Isaiah 53:1-7, emphasis added).

This striking prophecy was penned nearly 700 years before Jesus Christ was born in Bethlehem, and it was fulfilled perfectly when He hung upon the cross. On that fateful day outside Jerusalem, "*He was led as a lamb to the slaughter.*" Isaiah also clarified, "The Lord has laid on Him the iniquity of us all." This means that Jesus not only mysteriously bore within His Divine Person the sins of Adam, Eve, Cain, Abel, Noah, Abraham, Jonah, and David, but those of Julius Caesar, Constantine, Napoleon, George Washington, Adolph Hitler, Marilyn Monroe, George Bush, Osama bin Laden, Saddam Hussein, Britney Spears, and Madonna—including your sins and mine. He is the "Savior of the world" (1 John 4:14) who bore the sins of every person who has lived upon planet Earth, or who will live, from the days of Adam to the end of time. On a Friday afternoon, after six hours of horrific agony that can never be fully understood by mortal man, Jesus Christ finally cried out, "It is finished! And bowing His head, He gave up His spirit" (John 19:30). *Then He died.*

This entire drama can only be understood in the light of the Book of Genesis. To quickly summarize what we've seen so far: In the beginning, God created our world. He formed man from the dust of the ground. Planting two special trees in the Garden of Eden, He gave Adam a choice to obey or disobey. "You will surely die," the Creator warned. This would be the consequence of sin. "You will not surely die," countered lucifer through the snake. After Adam and Eve ate the forbidden fruit, God sadly announced that they would "return to the ground," then He posted Cherubim warriors with flaming swords "to guard the way to the tree of life" so that fallen man could not "eat, and live forever" in his fallen state. Without heavenly help, man was doomed.

Thankfully, mercy extended its scepter. Animals were killed. Coats of skin were made. Adam and Eve's nakedness was covered, even before their eviction from Paradise. All throughout Old Testament history, humanity waited for its Messiah to come. Finally, the Predicted One arrived. In fulfillment of ancient prophecies, Jesus Christ was "led as a lamb to the slaughter." During history's darkest—and most glorious—hour, on a day millions call "Good Friday," our Savior trumpeted, "It is finished!" Bearing the sins of the entire world, He breathed His last breath. God's first Edenic warning, "You will surely die," was uniquely executed upon His own Son. Jesus bore "the iniquity of us all." Like the first lamb slain in Eden, He took our place. He died for us.

The New Testament is exceedingly clear that Jesus *really did die.* This fact is the cornerstone of the "gospel," which means the "Good News." Here is what God's Book says:

> *Moreover, brethren, I declare to you the gospel which I preached to you, which also you received and in which you stand, by which also you are saved, if you hold fast that word which I preached to you—unless you*

believed in vain. For I delivered to you first of all that which I also received: that **Christ died for our sins** *according to the Scriptures* (1 Corinthians 15:1-3).

"*Christ died for our sins.*" This is what Paul boldly preached, and what we are to firmly believe, receive, stand upon, and hold onto. This is the message "by which also you are saved." It's life or death. Again, Paul wrote:

But God demonstrates His own love toward us, in that while we were still sinners, **Christ died for us** (Romans 5:8, emphasis added).

But we see Jesus, who was made a little lower than the angels, for the suffering of death crowned with glory and honor, that He, by the grace of God, might **taste death for everyone** (Hebrews 2:9, emphasis added).

On that Friday afternoon at approximately 3:00 P.M., the agony of Jesus Christ finally ceased. At last, after unimaginable suffering, He was dead. Devastated disciples, heartbroken friends, sneering enemies, proud priests, corrupt rulers, holy angels, and deceptive devils all witnessed this cosmic event. They were there at the Cross. A friend of mine once told me that he had the unusual experience of praying with a group of Christians for another man present who was demon-possessed. "In the name of Jesus Christ," my friend commanded the unclean spirit, "Come out of him! You were defeated at the cross!" Before the demons left the possessed man's body, a snarling voice replied, "How do you know? Were you there? I was. *We were all there at the Cross!*" My friend told me he would never forget those words.

On that fateful Friday nearly 2,000 years ago, two criminals were also crucified next to Jesus, with the Savior's Cross in the middle. After 3:00 P.M., because "the Sabbath drew near" (Luke 23:54), certain Jewish priests wanted to make sure "that the bodies should not remain on the cross on the Sabbath...[so] the Jews asked Pilate [the Roman governor] that their legs might be broken, and that they might be taken away" (John 19:31). It's amazing that these men were so conscientious about keeping the Sabbath, yet they had no qualms about crucifying the Son of God! Nevertheless, at their request:

> *Then the soldiers came and broke the legs of the first and of the other who was crucified with Him.* **But when they came to Jesus and saw that He was already dead, they did not break His legs.** *But one of the soldiers pierced His side with a spear, and immediately blood and water came out. And he who has seen has testified, and his testimony is true; and he knows that he is telling the truth, so that you may believe. For these things were done that the Scripture should be fulfilled, "Not one of His bones shall be broken." And again another Scripture says, "They shall look on Him whom they pierced"* (John 19:32-37, emphasis added).

This proves that Jesus Christ was actually dead. If even a tiny spark of life remained in Him, the Roman soldiers would have broken His legs to prevent any possible escape. But when "they came to Jesus [they] saw that He was already dead." In an unusual act, to remove any lingering doubt, one soldier pierced His side with a spear. Blood and water gushed from the gaping wound, but there was no movement. Christ hung motionless and breathless, suspended between heaven and earth.

> *After this, Joseph of Arimathea, being a disciple of Jesus, but secretly, for fear of the Jews, asked Pilate that he might take away the body of Jesus; and Pilate gave him permission. So he came and took the body of Jesus* (John 19:38).

Joseph of Arimathea, Mary the mother of Jesus, certain women, and other grief-stricken disciples, slowly "took the body of Jesus" off the cross. Someone must have pulled out the nails, one by one, as others sorrowfully wiped blood from His forehead, back, hands, arms, chest, legs, and feet. Crucifixion is a gruesome way to die. Consider how Christ's mother must have felt! Her mind must have been flooded with memories. I'm sure she wailed loudly as she remembered cradling and nursing her baby boy 33 years earlier. Throughout His babyhood, childhood, youth, and manhood, Jesus had been so full of life! No one was like Him! Now His eyes stared vacantly into space—just like the eyes of that first bleeding lamb Adam killed with his own hands.

The two deaths are connected. The first lamb was a shadow. The second Lamb was the fulfillment. If Adam had only known that all of this would happen, he would never have eaten that fruit!

Then they took the body of Jesus, and bound it in strips of linen with the spices, as the custom of the Jews is to bury. Now in the place where He was crucified there was a garden, and in the garden a new tomb in which no one had yet been laid. So there they laid Jesus, because of the Jews' Preparation Day, for the tomb was nearby (John 19:40-42).

A mournful caravan of His closest followers slowly carried the Savior's lifeless body toward a rock tomb cut into the side of a hill. *Why did this happen?* They must have wondered. *We never thought it would end like this!* Crossing the tomb's threshold and entering its dreary darkness, they sorrowfully laid the body of Jesus Christ on a rocky bed prepared for His beaten and battered form. Moments passed. More silence. *This is it,* they moaned. "Goodbye, Jesus!" "We'll always love You." "We appreciate everything You did for us." "Oh God, please help us! What shall we do now?" One by one, they left. Perhaps His mother was the last to leave. She probably had to be carried out. When they were all outside, a group of men rolled a heavy stone over the entrance to the cave. Then they all returned to their homes, fully believing that they would never see their Best Friend again.

Friday night slowly wore on and was replaced by daylight. Did Christ's small band of followers attend synagogue services the next day? Probably not. It would have been too painful to face a crowd; especially if some of their dead

Master's gloating enemies were present. Sabbath afternoon shifted into evening again, and then Saturday night's darkest hours slowly gave way to the dawning of another apparently normal day. Sunday morning had arrived.

Unknown to human beings on earth, innumerable heavenly angels had been anxiously awaiting the signal: Five...four...three...two...one... Then God's voice may have thundered from beyond the stars, "It's time! Gabriel, GO!" Moving faster than a flash of lightning, an unidentified flying object suddenly entered earth's upper atmosphere. Unseen by man, it soared with incalculable speed toward the Middle East, toward the land of Israel, toward the city of Jerusalem. Its target: a stone covering a tomb cut deep in rock. The Scripture records:

> Now after the Sabbath, as the first day of the week began to dawn, Mary Magdalene and the other Mary came to see the tomb. And behold, there was a great earthquake; for an angel of the Lord descended from heaven, and came and rolled back the stone from the door, and sat on it. His countenance was like lightning, and his clothing as white as snow (Matthew 28:1-3).

Satan's entire host would have prevented the event if they could, but this was impossible. Lucifer feared the worst, for he had studied the prophecies too. Isaiah chapter 53 predicted that even though Israel's Messiah would "make His soul an offering for sin" (verse 10), *this was not the end.* The rest of the verse cryptically announced, "*He shall see His seed,* He shall prolong His days, and the pleasure of the Lord shall prosper in His hand." The devil trembled. *Aghh! No, not the resurrection!*

The women who returned to the rocky tomb on Sunday morning were completely clueless. In fact, all of the disciples were woefully ignorant of what was about to occur, even though Jesus Christ had predicted it many times during His three and a half years of public ministry. Months before the crucifixion, Luke reported:

*Then He took the twelve aside and said to them, "Behold, we are going up to Jerusalem, and all things that are written by the prophets concerning the Son of Man will be accomplished. For He will be delivered to the Gentiles and will be mocked and insulted and spit upon. **They will scourge Him and kill Him. And the third day He will rise again.**" But they understood none of these things; this saying was hidden from them, and they did not know the things which were spoken* (Luke 18:31-34, emphasis added).

The reason this crucifixion-resurrection announcement was "hidden" from Christ's disciples—even though He told them—was because unseen influences had blinded their minds. Lucifer made sure of it. The very idea of a resurrection from the dead terrified the prince of darkness. "Don't even speak of it!" He may have instructed his demons. Whenever the Master brought it up, satan opposed it relentlessly (see Matt. 16:21-23). But Jesus kept teaching it. He was emphatic that His enemies would "kill Him," yet on "the third day He will rise again."

On Sunday morning, as the women approached the tomb, "they said among themselves, 'Who will roll away the stone from the door of the tomb for us?'" (Mark 16:3). As they neared its rocky entrance, they were amazed to discover that the stone had already been rolled away! *Has someone stolen our Lord's body?* they wondered. Terrified and bewildered, they crossed the cave's threshold and entered the tomb's damp darkness to see for themselves. "They went in and did not find the body of the Lord Jesus" (Luke 24:3). "What has happened?" they asked each other in shocked disbelief. "What does it all mean?" Luke informs us:

And it happened, as they were greatly perplexed about this, that behold, two men stood by them in shining garments. Then, as they were afraid and bowed their faces to the earth, they said to them, "Why do you seek the living among the dead? He is not here, but is risen! Remember how

He spoke to you when He was still in Galilee, saying, 'The Son of Man must be delivered into the hands of sinful men, and be crucified, and the third day rise again.'" And they remembered His words (Luke 24:4-8).

This section should be carefully analyzed. Those "two men" in "shining garments" were holy angels in human form. They appeared from the Other Side. Guided by enlightened angelic intelligence, they understood the mystery of death, burial, and resurrection. Veiling their heavenly glory so they could appear before mortal eyes, they asked the women, "Why do you seek the living among the dead?" Take note of this. Those angels recognized a sharp distinction between "the living" and "the dead." From 3:00 P.M. on Friday afternoon until early Sunday morning, our Savior was "among the dead." For three days He had been resting lifeless and motionless, without breath, heartbeat, sight or sound, inside a dark, dismal, clammy cave. But no longer. The angel said, "He is not here, but is risen!" Now He was among "the living" once again!

Let's take a quick survey of a few more New Testament passages about the death, burial, and resurrection of Jesus Christ from the dead. During His public ministry, the Lord Himself taught these truths to His disciples:

*From that time Jesus began to show to His disciples that He must go to Jerusalem, and suffer many things from the elders and chief priests and scribes, and **be killed, and be raised the third day*** (Matthew 16:21, emphasis added).

Holy angels proclaimed His resurrection to the women on Sunday morning:

*But the angel answered and said to the women, "Do not be afraid, for I know that you seek Jesus who was crucified. He is not here; **for He is risen,** as He said. Come, see the place where the Lord lay"* (Matthew 28:5-6, emphasis added).

Paul preached the saving message of Jesus Christ's death, burial, and resurrection:

*For I delivered to you first of all that which I also received: that **Christ**
*died for our sins** according to the Scriptures, and that **He was buried**,*
*and that **He rose again** the third day according to the Scriptures*
(1 Corinthians 15:3-4, emphasis added).

When a there-is-no-resurrection heresy entered the early Christian Church, Paul opposed it vigorously. He contended forcefully:

*Now if Christ is preached that He has been raised from the dead, **how**
*do some among you say that there is no resurrection of dead?** But if*
there is no resurrection of the dead, then Christ is not risen. And if Christ
is not risen, then our preaching is empty, and your faith is also empty. ...
***But now Christ is risen from the dead,** and has become the firstfruits*
of those who have fallen asleep (1 Corinthians 15:12-14, 20, emphasis
added).

The Book of Revelation is the Bible's last book, and it is the greatest book on prophecy ever written. The aged disciple John, who was at that time a prisoner of the Roman Empire on a Greek island called Patmos, penned it. Somewhere around the year A.D. 96, Jesus Christ, the Risen One, made a personal appearance to His incarcerated servant. Notice carefully the Savior's own words spoken to His faithful follower, and to us. The Lord announced:

*I am He who **lives**, and was **dead**, and behold, I am **alive** forevermore.*
Amen. And I have the keys of Hades and of Death (Revelation 1:18,
emphasis added).

*These things says the First and the Last, who was **dead**, and **came to life*** (Revelation 2:8, emphasis added).

These authoritative pronouncements recorded in the last book of the Bible come from the divine lips of Jesus Christ Himself. If anyone knows the truth about the mysteries of life, death, and the afterlife—it's Him, for to quote a popular phrase, He's "been there and done that." Using words that parallel perfectly those spoken by heavenly angels to the women who discovered an empty tomb, the Resurrected One also made a razor sharp distinction between the living and the dead. Twice He informed John that He *"was dead."* It's the truth. *Jesus was really dead!* But then He revealed the message that has become the cornerstone of every human being's hope of eternal life. *"Behold, I am alive forevermore."* On Sunday morning, He "came to life." Hallelujah!

In the light of these plain "I was dead but am alive forevermore" statements from the lips of the Son of God in the Book of Revelation, let's return once again to the original subject matter of this book—talking to the dead.

We're not done yet.

ENDNOTE

1.   Taken from a song entitled, *The Caretakers*, written by Vince Christian. Music by Charles Lawson.

Chapter 10

JERUSALEM SÉANCE

The more original a discovery, the more obvious it seems afterwards.

—Arthur Koestler (1905-1983), British novelist

ALLOW me to indulge your imagination with a fictitious, yet highly pertinent, illustration. It's Friday night, nearly 2,000 years ago, and two grief-stricken women are talking together inside a Jerusalem residence. "I can't believe that Jesus is really dead!" Lydia moaned.

"I know," Rivka replied, "the last 24 hours make no sense, no sense at all!"

"We all thought that Jesus of Nazareth was the true Messiah," Lydia continued, "who would free us from the Romans and rule over all nations from Jerusalem. At least, that's what our Rabbis told us would happen when God's Messiah came. Now, our hopes are dashed! Less than five hours ago, we watched Him die."

"I have so many questions," Rivka stammered helplessly. "I wish we could still talk to Jesus!"

After a long pause, Lydia whispered quietly, *"Maybe we can."*

"What! How?" Rivka questioned incredulously.

"Well, there's an old woman who lives in the Solomon section of East Jerusalem, on the corner of Eighth and Pomegranate. Rumor has it that she is a medium...you know, someone who talks to dead people. Most of my friends raise their eyebrows at her profession, but my mom thinks she's the real deal. Perhaps...just maybe...she can make contact with the spirit of Jesus of Nazareth. What do you think? Should we try to find her?"

After a few seconds of awkward silence, Rivka stuttered nervously, "Err, ah...I...I don't know...but...I sure have lots of questions...well, why not? Let's give it a try!"

Grabbing their shawls, the two women were quickly on their way toward Eighth and Pomegranate. Soon they arrived in front of a small, dingy-looking residence with no windows in the front. A lone dog howled somewhere in the neighborhood beneath a full moon. *Knock...knock...knock...*

Moments later, faint shuffling was heard inside the house. "Who is it?" an elderly voice asked from behind the door.

"It's me, Lydia, and my friend Rivka. I think you know my mother, Rachel. Can we talk to you?"

There was silence for a moment, then sounds of a chain being unlocked, then a creaky door slowly opened about a foot. "I'm Ariella," said the old woman in the opening, "How can I help you?"

Lydia quietly explained the reason for their visit. Ariella let them in. The two younger women were then led down a narrow corridor, past an eating room, around a corner, around another corner, and then into a small room lit by eight flickering candles, in the midst of which stood a table and four chairs. A bowl of herbs was on the table, along with a few shiny rocks, some dried flowers, a bowl of figs, and an olive branch. The three women sat down.

"Who do you want me to contact?" the medium asked quietly.

"Jesus of Nazareth," Lydia replied. "Perhaps you've heard of Him. He was a noble, compassionate man, who even performed miracles. Many of us were sure He was the long-awaited Messiah of Israel. But...," lowering her voice, Lydia continued, "He had many enemies within the Sanhedrin...."

Ariella nodded understandably.

Lydia paused again, becoming teary-eyed, "He was turned over to Pontius Pilate, and then the Romans crucified Him this morning, along with two thieves. He died at about the ninth hour."

Lydia caught the reflection of flickering candles in Ariella's dark eyes that, within seconds, closed tightly. No one moved. Ariella quietly muttered words neither Lydia nor Rivka could understand. Minutes passed. The neighborhood dog howled again. Suddenly, directly above the only remaining empty chair around the table, an eerie mist appeared, which slowly formed itself into the face and upper body of a man. Lydia and Rivka gasped, recognizing the face instantly. The likeness was unmistakable! It was the ghost of Jesus of Nazareth!

That's enough. I'll end my fictitious illustration here. Now here's the key question: Could something like this have really occurred? Could the ghost, spirit, or disembodied soul of the real Jesus of Nazareth have made an actual appearance inside a candlelit room sometime between Friday afternoon and Sunday morning while His physical body rested silently in Joseph's tomb? Let's discuss this.

First, we already know what the Bible says about mediums and spiritists, thus Lydia and Rivka should never have visited the corner of Eighth and Pomegranate in the first place. Second, Ariella—a practicing medium—was in the wrong profession, and her activities are pointedly labeled "an abomination" in God's Book. Third, according to the literal language of the New

Testament, it was Jesus Christ Himself, not just His physical body, who "died" on Friday afternoon and was "dead" until Sunday morning.

Again, notice the exact language of Scripture. Paul wrote, "*Christ died* for our sins, according to the Scriptures" (1 Cor. 15:3, emphasis added). The text doesn't say, "Christ's *body* died," but rather, "*Christ died.*" After His resurrection, the Risen One announced to John, "*I am He who lives, and was dead*, and behold, *I am alive* forevermore" (Rev. 1:18, emphasis added). In this passage, Jesus Christ was plainly talking about His Person. He said He "was dead," then He said, "I am alive forevermore." These are the words of the Resurrected One.

Fourth, let's take another look at what the New Testament teaches about *where* Jesus Christ was between Friday afternoon and Sunday morning. The section we shall consider is found in the Book of Acts, chapter 2, verses 22-32, which lies at the heart of a sermon preached by Peter on the Day of Pentecost. On that eventful day, more than on any previous day in his entire life, Peter was "filled with the Holy Spirit" (Acts 2:4). His words were 100% inspired. Here's what this Spirit-anointed man boldly proclaimed to a crowd of over 3,000 wide-eyed listeners:

> *Men of Israel, hear these words: Jesus of Nazareth, a Man attested by God to you by miracles, wonders, and signs which God did through Him in your midst, as you yourselves also know—Him, being delivered by the determined purpose and foreknowledge of God, you have taken by lawless hands, have crucified, and put to death; whom God raised up, having loosed the pains of death, because it was not possible that He should be held by it. For David says concerning Him:*

> *"I foresaw the Lord always before my face,*
> *For He is at my right hand, that I may not be shaken.*
> *Therefore my heart rejoiced, and my tongue was glad;*

Moreover my flesh also will rest in hope.
For You will not leave my soul in Hades,
Nor will You allow Your Holy One to see corruption.
You have made known to me the ways of life;
You will make me full of joy in Your presence."

Men and brethren, let me speak freely to you of the patriarch David, that he is both dead and buried, and his tomb is with us to this day. Therefore, being a prophet, and knowing that God had sworn with an oath to him that of the fruit of his body, according to the flesh, He would raise up the Christ to sit on his throne, he, foreseeing this, spoke concerning the resurrection of the Christ, **that His soul was not left in Hades, nor did His flesh see corruption.** *This Jesus God has raised up, of which we are all witnesses* (Acts 2:22-32, emphasis added).

Peter was preaching to a crowd of astonished Jews about the life, death, burial, and resurrection of Jesus Christ, and about how these remarkable events fulfilled what David—Israel's greatest king—had originally written nearly 1,000 years earlier in Psalm 16:8-11. *"You will not leave my soul in Hades,"* King David declared, *"nor will You allow Your Holy One to see corruption"* (Ps. 16:10). In his Pentecostal message, Peter applied David's words, not to the Jewish king himself, but to Israel's Messiah. "David...being a prophet...*spoke concerning the resurrection of the Christ, that His soul was not left in Hades, nor did His flesh see corruption.*" It must be so, for on the Day of Pentecost Peter said that King David was "both dead and buried, and his tomb is with us to this day." David's "flesh" did "see corruption."

Let's analyze Peter's message closely. First, Peter said that Jesus Christ's "soul was not left in *Hades.*" The Greek word, *Hades,* sometimes translated "hell" (KJV), literally means "the grave." This was where Christ's "soul" resided between Friday and Sunday. *"His soul was not left in Hades,"* Peter said.

Earlier we noted that when God first created Adam from the dust of the ground, "man became a living soul" (Gen. 2:7). In Genesis 2:7, the word "soul" applied, not to a disembodied ghost, *but to Adam's entire person*. Similarly, when Peter said that Jesus Christ's "soul was not left in Hades," this simply means that His entire Person was not left in the grave for very long.

Now notice: Christ's soul was not "left" there. The word "left" proves that Jesus Christ's "soul," or person, was entirely passive during that woeful period. If His body had remained in the tomb any longer than three days, it would have seen "corruption," rotted, and become food for worms. But it didn't. Peter concluded, "This Jesus God has raised up, of which we are all witnesses."

This answers the question of where Jesus Christ was between Friday and Sunday. According to Matthew, Mark, Luke, John, King David, the apostle Peter, and the rest of the New Testament, *He was dead, in Joseph's tomb, waiting for His Father to raise Him up*. Peter concluded, "This Jesus God has raised up, of which we are all witnesses."

Now let's return to that Jerusalem séance. According to the Holy Bible, contacting the dead is forbidden (see Deut. 18:11), mediumship is condemned (see Lev. 20:6), and Jesus Christ Himself—His "soul"—rested quietly inside a rocky tomb from Friday to Sunday (see Acts 2:31; Luke 23:52-53). Thus it would have been *impossible* for Jesus to mystically "appear" to Lydia, Rivka, and Ariella above that fourth chair, even if He wanted to (which He didn't).

Let me clarify. It's true, an "appearance" might have occurred, but it would not have been the ghost of the real Jesus Christ of Nazareth that materialized. Never! It would have been a demon in disguise, similar to the one who impersonated Samuel before Saul in the dark cave at Endor.

Sylvia Browne, one of the 21st century's most popular mediums, believes that the "spirit" of Jesus Christ of Nazareth did "appear" many times from the Other Side. In *Visits From the Afterlife*, Browne wrote:

In fact, depending on which of the twenty-six versions of the Bible you read, Jesus Himself appeared on earth in spirit form between six and ten times after He ascended. Paul's first letter to the Corinthians, for example, in the Revised Standard Edition, Chapter 15, verses 3-8, reads, "...that Christ died for our sins..., that He was buried, that He was raised on the third day..., and that He appeared to more than five hundred brethren at once.... Then He appeared to James, then to all the apostles.... He appeared also to me." With these and other Biblical accounts of the earthly *appearances of a Spirit who had very definitely transcended the Other Side*, how and why would someone get the idea that encounters between humankind and the afterlife are evil? I'm certainly not about to give credit to a supposed "devil" for Christ's visitations to this world after His crucifixion, are you? [1]

I don't question Browne's sincerity, but honestly, these are the kind of paragraphs that can easily deceive those who are merely surface readers of God's Book. Here's the entire text, as Paul actually wrote it:

> *For I delivered to you first of all that which I also received: that Christ died for our sins according to the Scriptures, and that He was buried, and that He rose again the third day according to the Scriptures, and that He was seen by Cephas* [Peter], *then by the twelve. After that He was seen by over five hundred brethren at once, of whom the greater part remain to the present, but some have fallen asleep. After that He was seen by James, then by all the apostles. Then last of all He was seen by me also, as by one born out of due time* (1 Corinthians 15:3-8).

These verses simply tell us that Jesus Christ died, was buried, rose from the dead, and that after His resurrection He personally appeared to Peter, then to the rest of the disciples, then to over 500 of His followers, then to James, then again to all of His disciples, and finally to Paul himself. There is no hint in First Corinthians 15 that these appearances were anything other than those of *a physically resurrected Man in bodily form.*

Immediately after His resurrection, Jesus Christ's first "appearance" was to Mary Magdalene outside the tomb. Here's the biblical account:

> But Mary stood outside by the tomb weeping, and as she wept she stooped down and looked into the tomb. And she saw two angels in white sitting, one at the head and the other at the feet, where the body of Jesus had lain. Then they said to her, "Woman, why are you weeping?" She said to them, "Because they have taken away my Lord, and I do not know where they have laid Him." Now when she had said this, she turned around and saw Jesus standing there, and did not know that it was Jesus. Jesus said to her, "Woman, why are you weeping? Whom are you seeking?" She, supposing Him to be the gardener, said to Him, "Sir, if You have carried Him away, tell me where You have laid Him, and I will take Him away." Jesus said to her, "Mary!" She turned and said to Him, "Rabboni!" (which is to say, Teacher). Jesus said to her, "Do not cling to Me, for I have not yet ascended to My Father; but go to My brethren and say to them, 'I am ascending to My Father and your Father, and to My God and your God.'" Mary Magdalene came and told the disciples that she had seen the Lord, and that He had spoken these things to her (John 20:11-18).

Here Jesus appeared as a resurrected Man, not a spirit. Overwhelmed with joy, Mary either gave Him a big hug, or knelt down and grasped His legs. Christ tenderly responded, *"Do not cling to Me,* for I have not yet ascended to My Father." It's impossible to "cling" to a ghost. The Savior's words, "I have not yet ascended to My Father," reveal that He had not yet been to Heaven, but that He was anxious to go there shortly (probably to make sure His sacrifice was accepted by His Father—which it most certainly was). Soon after this first "appearance" to Mary, Jesus appeared to His disciples. Here's Luke account:

Now as they said these things, Jesus Himself stood in the midst of them, and said to them, "Peace to you." But they were terrified and frightened, and supposed they had seen a spirit. And He said to them, "Why are you troubled? And why do doubts arise in your hearts? Behold My hands and My feet, that it is I Myself. Handle Me and see, for a spirit does not have flesh and bones as you see I have." When He had said this, He showed them His hands and His feet. But while they still did not believe for joy, and marveled, He said to them, "Have you any food here?" So they gave Him a piece of a broiled fish and some honeycomb. And He took it and ate in their presence (Luke 24:36-43).

It was "Jesus Himself" who "stood" there. At first, the disciples "were terrified and frightened, and supposed they had seen a spirit." They knew what the Bible teaches about familiar spirits and demons. Thinking this was a demon in disguise, they were scared out of their wits. Then their Risen Lord brought clarity with the gracious invitation, "Behold My hands and My feet, that it is I Myself." They saw the nail scars in His wrists, and the holes in His feet.

"Handle Me and see," Jesus continued, *"for a spirit does not have flesh and bones as you see I have."* As final proof, Jesus took a piece of cooked fish, and "ate in their presence." Each detail of this account is significant. From hands, to feet, to fish, Jesus Christ systematically worked, step by step, act by act, proof by proof, to demonstrate to all ages that He was a resurrected Man, not a ghost. He would leave no cracks open for demonic deception.

Every post-resurrection appearance of Jesus Christ prior to His ascension to Heaven was absolutely physical. Here is Luke's description of how He returned to God:

Now when He had spoken these things, while they watched, He was taken up, and a cloud received Him out of their sight. And while they looked steadfastly toward heaven as He went up, behold, two men stood by them in white apparel, who also said, "Men of Galilee, why do you stand gazing up into heaven? This same Jesus, who was taken up from you into heaven, will so come in like manner as you saw Him go into heaven" (Acts 1:9-11).

Jesus Christ's ascension was literal, visible, and physical. His followers "watched" the entire event. Then "behold, two men stood by them in white apparel." These weren't ghosts or demons, but holy angels in human form. "This same Jesus," they commented, "who was taken up from you into heaven, *will so come in like manner as you saw Him go into heaven.*" The truth is that Jesus Christ ascended to Heaven as a real Man, that He's there now as a real Man, and that He will someday return as a real Man. That's what the angels said. Surely they had their theology straight.

After His ascension, Jesus Christ did appear a few other times to select individuals—to Stephen (see Acts 7:55-56), to Paul (see Acts 9:1-6), and to John on the island of Patmos (see Rev. 1:12-17); but He never appeared as a spirit or ghost; always as a real person. And every time, these appearances were the result of Jesus Christ giving "a vision" to those who saw Him. Here's one example:

*Now the Lord spoke to Paul in the night **by a vision,** "Do not be afraid, but speak, and do not keep silent; for I am with you, and no one will attack you to hurt you; for I have many people in this city"* (Acts 18:9-10, emphasis added).

Thus every time Jesus Christ appeared on earth after He had "risen from the dead" (Matt. 28:7), it was as a resurrected Man in bodily form. Then after His ascension to Heaven, His subsequent appearances were always by "a vision." In the clear light of these plain biblical facts, let's look again at what Sylvia Browne wrote in her *Visits From the Afterlife*:

> With these and other Biblical accounts of the earthly *appearances of a Spirit who had very definitely transcended the Other Side*, how and why would someone get the idea that encounters between humankind and the afterlife are evil? I'm certainly not about to give credit to a supposed "devil" for Christ's visitations to this world after His crucifixion, are you? [2]

These words amaze me! The fact is that there are *no* biblical accounts of Jesus ever appearing as "a Spirit" to anyone, not even once. The Savior Himself said to His disciples after His resurrection, "Handle Me and see, for a spirit does not have flesh and bones as you see I have." Browne inquired, "*Why* would someone get the idea that encounters between humankind and the afterlife are evil?" Why? Because God's Word plainly warns about "deceiving spirits" (1 Tim. 4:1), that's why. Finally, Browne asked, "I'm certainly not about to give credit to a supposed 'devil' for Christ's visitations to this world after His crucifixion, are you?" No; not for His true "visitations" as described in the Bible. But I do give credit to a real devil for convincing millions that he doesn't exist. Remember, Sylvia Browne is a spiritualist medium who not only denies satan's existence, but who also conducts séances.[3] Because she claims to believe God's Book, I would ask her: Who spoke through the snake in Eden? Who tempted Jesus in the desert? Who plunged 2,000 pigs into the sea? Whatever she might say, the Bible's answer is clear. It was "the devil and his angels" (see Matt. 25:41).

Jesus Christ warned:

Take heed that no one deceives you (Matthew 24:4).

Paul warned:

Let no one deceive you by any means (2 Thessalonians 2:3).

Peter warned:

But there were also false prophets among the people, even as there will be ***false teachers*** *among you* (2 Peter 2:1, emphasis added).

John warned:

The devil, who deceived them, was cast into the lake of fire and brimstone... (Revelation 20:10).

With solemn warnings like these about being deceived by satan and false teachers, it behooves each of us to make sure that what we believe is really what the Bible actually says. "What is right is not always popular," someone once observed, "and what is popular is not always right." How true this is!

You may be shocked to read this, but it's a fact that there is not one solitary instance in the entire Bible where an authentic disembodied spirit or ghost of a dead person has legitimately appeared from the Other Side. The only section in the Old Testament that has been interpreted as a bona fide after-death encounter is the account of King Saul visiting a witch at Endor. We have already explored this. That was a demon in disguise. But there is one other passage in the New Testament that now demands our attention. It's the story of how Moses and Elijah "appeared" before Jesus Christ on a mountain. Here's Luke's description of the event:

"But I [Jesus] tell you truly, there are some standing here who shall not taste death till they see the kingdom of God." Now it came to pass, about eight days after these sayings, that He took Peter, John, and James and went up on the mountain to pray. As He prayed, the appearance of His face was altered, and His robe became white and glistening. And behold,

two men talked with Him, who were Moses and Elijah, who appeared in glory and spoke of His decease which He was about to accomplish at Jerusalem. But Peter and those with him were heavy with sleep; and when they were fully awake, they saw His glory and the two men who stood with Him. Then it happened, as they were parting from Him, that Peter said to Jesus, "Master, it is good for us to be here; and let us make three tabernacles: one for You, one for Moses, and one for Elijah"—not knowing what he said. While he was saying this, a cloud came and overshadowed them; and they were fearful as they entered the cloud. And a voice came out of the cloud, saying, "This is My beloved Son. Hear Him!" When the voice had ceased, Jesus was found alone. But they kept quiet, and told no one in those days any of the things they had seen (Luke 9:27-36).

Does this mean that the ghosts of two dead people—Moses and Elijah—appeared to Jesus Christ, Peter, James, and John from the Other Side? If so, then this is the only such account in the entire Bible, for there is no other. In the *Star Wars* movie series, the deceased Obi-Wan Kenobi did appear to Luke Skywalker—but you won't find anything like this in God's Book. So what about Moses and Elijah?

Luke 9:27-36 isn't as difficult to understand as one might think. First of all, Luke specified that it was *"two men"*—not two ghosts—who appeared to Jesus and His disciples on that lonely mountain. Second, the Old Testament prophet Elijah never died; rather, he was translated directly into Heaven without tasting death. "Then it happened, as they [Elijah and Elisha] continued on and talked, that suddenly a chariot of fire appeared with horses of fire, and separated the two of them; *and Elijah went up by a whirlwind into heaven*" (2 Kings 2:11, emphasis added). Elijah "went up" physically and bodily, just like Jesus Christ ascended after His resurrection. Therefore, as far as Elijah goes, he never died and was not dead. When he came down from Heaven to meet Jesus on the mountain, he simply "appeared in glory."

The controversial appearance is that of "Moses." The Old Testament is clear that at the end of his lengthy career, Moses "died" and was "buried" (Deut. 34:5-6). So how could he "appear" over a thousand years later to Jesus? The solution to this dilemma is found the New Testament Book of Jude. Here's what Jude wrote:

> *Yet Michael the archangel, in contending with the devil,* **when he disputed about the body of Moses,** *dared not bring against him a reviling accusation, but said, "The Lord rebuke you!"* (Jude 9, emphasis added).

Jude tells us that sometime after Moses "died" and was "buried," "Michael the archangel" descended from Heaven and, "contending with the devil...he disputed about the body of Moses." Michael must have visited the exact location of Moses' grave. Once there, he wanted "the body of Moses." Then satan showed up, and he must have said something like, "Forget it! You can't take him. Moses is mine!" Michael didn't argue, but simply countered with, "The Lord rebuke you!"

This unusual dialog makes sense only if "Michael the archangel" had come to resurrect "the body of Moses" in God's name prior to the general resurrection of the saints. Why would Michael do this? Just think about it. Moses was close to God. He led Israel out of Egypt, beheld the Lord's glory on Mount Sinai, personally received the Ten Commandments, and led God's people for 40 years through a desolate wilderness. Yet in spite of his faithfulness, Moses committed one major sin at the entrance of Canaan (see Num. 20) that resulted in his being denied access into an earthly Promised Land (see Deut. 32:48-52). Moses longed to enter that land, but God said no. Unknown to this godly man, the Lord must have decided to honor him above all earthly expectations.

So, sometime after Moses died and was buried, God must have told Michael, "Go get him!"

Satan was furious! "Moses is a sinner! He's under my domain. You can't have him!"

But, by virtue of *the future death, burial, and resurrection of Jesus Christ from the dead*, the Lord acted early and essentially informed His enemy, "Moses is mine. Get out of My sight!" Satan lost the argument.

As far as we know, at that moment another first-time-ever event occurred. As we saw earlier, when Adam slew the lamb, this was the first time anything had ever died. "For dust you are, and to dust you shall return," was God's sentence against fallen humanity. But now, for the first time in human history, this sentence was about to be reversed. A mound of dust suddenly started moving beneath a silent tombstone somewhere near Mount Nebo. Again, both good and evil angels stood mesmerized, frozen in time, with eyes fixed on a patch of dirt. Then two feet, two hands, and an astonished face appeared! Moses was alive again! Then God took him to glory so that he could begin having eternal fellowship with his Maker and holy angels. After entering the pearly gates, Moses probably met Enoch too, for he had previously been translated without seeing death (see Gen. 5:23). Thousands of years later, Elijah joined them (see 2 Kings 2:11).

Now fast forward to the time of Luke 9, and put the pieces together. Jesus, Peter, James, and John are climbing a rugged "mountain to pray." Reaching the summit, Jesus drops to His knees. Night falls, His disciples slumber, yet Jesus prays on. Suddenly there is a burst of light! "The appearance of His face was altered, and His robe became white and glistening." Why this flood of heavenly glory? The reason is because, unknown to sinful mortals, history's greatest event is pending. Then, "behold, two men talked with Him, who were Moses and Elijah, who spoke of His decease which He was about to accomplish at Jerusalem." These were "two men," not see-through apparitions. It was a living, resurrected Moses, and a living, translated Elijah who appeared on that mountain.

Why did Moses and Elijah appear? Luke wrote that they came to speak to Jesus Christ about "His decease that He was about to accomplish at Jerusalem." "His decease" means His death. Jesus was soon to suffer the horrors of crucifixion just outside Jerusalem; and even worse, the hiding of His Father's face because of our sins (see Matt. 26:46). Although He was God's Son, He was now fully human, and He needed encouragement. Jesus had lived a lonely life for 33 years. No one on earth understood Him. "We didn't know who You was!" repeat the lyrics of a famous negro spiritual. He missed His Father, loyal angels, and probably Enoch, Moses, and Elijah, who He undoubtedly had an intimate relationship with before His birth in Bethlehem. Now He was a Man among men, and who better to lift His spirits than one man who had previously died and been raised to life; and another who, although his ministry had largely been rejected by ancient Israel (see 1 Kings 19:10), was nevertheless translated to glory without seeing death? The fit was perfect. "Go Moses, go Elijah! It's almost time!" thundered a voice beyond the stars.

But there's another reason why God chose those "two men." Immediately prior to their tiring trek up the mountainside, Jesus had informed His disciples, "There are some of you standing here who shall not taste death till they see the kingdom of God" (Luke 9:27). This statement puzzles many readers. What did Jesus mean?

Here's the answer: Just a few days later on that mountain summit, Peter, James, and John did see God's kingdom in miniature. First, Jesus Christ the King was there. Next, Moses was there who, because he had been physically resurrected, represented all of God's righteous saints who shall one day be resurrected at the return of Jesus Christ (more on this soon). Finally, there was Elijah who, because he had been translated without seeing death, represented God's "last generation" saints who would be taken to Heaven without tasting death at the end of the world. Paul described both groups when he wrote:

For the Lord Himself will descend from heaven with a shout, with the voice of an archangel, and with the trumpet of God. And **the dead in Christ** [the resurrected group] **will rise first.** *Then we who are alive* [the translated group] *and remain shall be caught up together with them in the clouds to meet the Lord in the air. And thus we shall always be with the Lord. Therefore comfort one another with these words* (1 Thessalonians 4:16-17, emphasis added).

Now the "Moses and Elijah" scene makes perfect sense. Jesus the King, a resurrected Moses, a translated Elijah—there was "the kingdom of God" in miniature. Our Savior needed this revelation before "His decease...at Jerusalem." He was soon to enter the darkness of Gethsemane, feel a kiss of betrayal from Judas, endure judicial trials before the Jewish Sanhedrin, King Herod, and Pontius Pilate, be mocked, whipped, beaten, and finally, crucified—the worst part of which was not the physical pain, but the agony of sensing an eternal separation from His Father because of our sins. O yes! Jesus needed encouragement! Soon He would suffer and die. Death is cold, dark, unfeeling, and ugly. But thank God, on the other side of death's door, Jesus would be raised to life.

I hope we have "laid to rest" any mistaken notion that either the Old Testament's Saul-in-the-cave encounter or the New Testament's Moses-and-Elijah appearance endorse any form of spiritualism, or the practice of talking to dead people. They don't. To interpret them thus is to "twist...the Scriptures" (see 2 Pet. 3:16) and to deny what God's Word says about necromancy. Again, you can search the Bible from Genesis to Revelation, but you won't find one solitary instance of any living human being talking to a dead person's ghost. It's just not there, no matter what Hollywood rolls out, or what modern mediums claim. Notice carefully what Job wrote so long ago:

As the cloud is consumed and vanisheth away: so he that goeth down to the grave shall come up no more. **He shall return no more to his house,** *neither shall his place know him any more* (Job 7:9-10 KJV, emphasis added).

This verse mentions the utter impossibility of a ghostly "return" from "the grave." "He that goeth down to the grave," Job clarified, "shall come up no more." Take note: *"He shall return no more to his house."* There it is. A dead man lying in his grave beneath his silent tombstone in a cemetery *cannot* come back to visit, or frighten, his living relatives. Such a thing is fundamentally impossible. That's what Job said. Thus all of the apparitions we read about earlier in this book could *not* have been the spirits of dead people.

Remember the spirit who visited Tom Murdic (Franklin, Tenn.), as reported in *People* magazine? "The ghost turns on appliances," Murdic said, "and bangs on walls but is otherwise, a good kid."[4] Such a noisy spirit! But can *a real dead person* cause such a ruckus? Not according to the Bible, for King David distinctly informs us:

> *The dead do not praise the Lord, nor any who go down **into silence*** (Psalm 115:17, emphasis added).

Thus the dead are *silent*, not rabble-rousers. What about Allison DuBois' story as reported in her best-selling autobiography, *Don't Kiss Them Goodbye*? The book's back cover declares:

> When she was six years old, Allison's deceased great-grandfather came to her with a message for her mother: "I am okay, I am still with you. Tell your mom there's no more pain.[5]

That otherworldly informant claimed to know many things about life on the Other Side. Was it really Allison's deceased great-grandfather who "came to her with a message for her mother"? Do dead people know such things? Not according to King Solomon who declared:

*For the living know that they will die; **but the dead know nothing**.*
...For there is no work or device or knowledge or wisdom in the grave
where you are going (Ecclesiastes 9:5,10, emphasis added).

All of these Bible verses—Job 7:9-10; Psalm 115:17; Ecclesiastes 9:5,10—
help us to understand why God so strongly forbids all forms of communication with dead people. The first reason is because such communication is
impossible. Have you heard the phrase, "Dead men don't tell tales?" It's the
truth. The second reason is because spiritualism itself is a direct doorway to
the demonic. Based on the above biblical statements, we know for sure that
Mr. Murdic's wall-banging resident and the apparition that appeared to
Allison DuBois were *not* who they appeared to be. The Bible unmasks these
diabolical tricksters who so cruelly take advantage of human grief. Now you
know exactly who they are. They're D.I.Ds: *Demons in Disguise.*

Here are two questions worth pondering as we close this chapter: Why
would satan and his legions go to such lengths to persuade human beings that
they are the spirits of dead people? And why has this dearly departed delusion
become so widespread *now*, more than ever before, to the point of flooding
Prime Time TV?

Is something apocalyptic afloat?

Let's find out.

ENDNOTES

1. Sylvia Browne, *Visits From the Afterlife* (London: New American
    Library, a division of Penguin books, 2003, 6, emphasis added.

2. Browne, *Visits*, 6, emphasis added.

3. Browne, *Visits*, 226.

4. "They See Dead People," *People* (November 7, 2005).

5.   Allison DuBois, *Don't Kiss Them Goodbye* (New York: Simon and Shuster, 2004, back cover text.

Chapter 11

ON THE ROAD TO ARMAGEDDON

This generation may be the one that will face Armageddon.

—Ronald Reagan (1911-2004),
40th President of the United States

Armageddon! This frightening apocalyptic word refers to Earth's last battle. Speculation has simmered for centuries about how close humanity is to this cosmic conflict, what contestants will be involved, what kind of battle will be fought and exactly where it will occur. Although many details remain foggy to Christians generally, it is becoming increasingly obvious that the day is rapidly approaching. The September 11, 2001 attack on the World Trade Center, Asia's deadly tsunami, hurricane Katrina, the global threat of Islamic radicals, and the terrorist race for a nuclear bomb—these all speak loudly to this generation. Many who read the Bible and watch Fox News can feel it coming. Armageddon looms on the horizon. When it hits, there's no escaping it.

Surprisingly, the word "Armageddon" is found only once in the Bible, in Revelation chapter 16, verse 16. The text says:

And they gathered them together to the place called in Hebrew,
Armageddon (Revelation 16:16, emphasis added).

Demons in Disguise isn't the place for a detailed study of every aspect of this end-of-the-age engagement (additional information is in my other book, *End Time Delusions*), but here I wish to highlight one major element firmly embedded within this mysterious prophecy: the unrecognized role of demonic spirits. The special activity of these dark forces, and their global influence, is specifically referred to immediately before the term "Armageddon" is mentioned. Notice carefully what the Book of Revelation distinctly predicts:

For they are spirits of demons, *performing signs, which go out to the kings of the earth and of the whole world, to gather them to the battle of that great day of God Almighty. "Behold, I am coming as a thief. Blessed is he who watches, and keeps his garments, lest he walk naked and they see his shame." And they gathered them together to the place called in Hebrew, Armageddon* (Revelation 16:14-16, emphasis added).

Let's unpack this startling revelation. Verse 14 predicts that the "spirits of demons" will prepare the world for the battle of "Armageddon" (verse 16). But as we've already discovered, demons don't often appear *as demons* before human beings. Instead, they hide their identity, wear masks, and are masters of disguise. "I'm not a demon," a real demon will contend earnestly, "but a friend." "God sent me," is one of their classic lines.

These six words, "For they are spirits of demons," contain heavenly intelligence information. They are God's attempt to lift the veil, penetrate the disguise, and to teach humanity the truth. Demonic spirits exist. They were originally created as noble, holy beings, but they went bad, sided with lucifer, and were evicted from glory. Throughout human history, starting among the leaves of a forbidden tree, they've been working diligently behind the scenes, pulling strings, weaving a web of lies, and seeking to carry out their infernal designs. There's no doubt they have a master plan. Their goal is global dominion. And you can be sure of this: One of their favorite strategies in their quest for a worldwide end-time takeover *is to disguise themselves as the ghosts of dead people.* And they can assume the form of anyone they wish: Marilyn Monroe, Elvis Presley, Princess Diana, or even the Virgin Mary.

This tactic worked against King Saul inside a cave at Endor. But that deception occurred at night, in the dark. For thousands of years the practice of necromancy has been largely scorned, being conducted mostly among the few. But in recent years this has changed dramatically—like never before. Because of highly rated TV series like "Medium" and "Ghost Whisperer", Hollywood movies like *White Noise* and *The Sixth Sense*, and professional mediums like Allison DuBois, John Edward, George Anderson, Carla Mae, Sylvia Browne, and Lisa Williams, who are not only best-selling authors but media stars, the net result is that communication with the dead has gone mainstream. We are not witnessing merely a social phenomenon. It's not just the ebb and flow of normal human events. Something larger is happening, something apocalyptic. The Book of Revelation predicted that this time would arrive. Now it's here. We're nearing Armageddon!

"They are spirits of demons, *performing signs...*" This forewarns us that during earth's final days a definite demonic strategy will be to perform "signs," or miracles. They have this capability. Demons perform signs in order to gain the confidence of their victims. When the "Seth" entity first manifested itself to Jane Roberts in New York in the 1960s, it performed a number of dramatic "signs" to prove it was who it claimed to be—the ghost of a dead person. "One witness, Robert Butts, said that [Jane's] hand began to change in appearance and resembled a paw." This was Seth's "sign." But this bizarre act doesn't really prove Seth's honesty, only his supernatural abilities.

A 1995 *Time* magazine cover story examining modern miracles concluded: "People are hungry for signs."[1] Demons realize this, which is why they often make noises in attics, fly forks, knives, and spoons through the air, knock pictures off walls, switch TV sets on and off, reveal information about the personal lives of the deceased, and even predict certain future events. These are all "signs" designed to convince skeptics that these activities are being performed by genuine, bona fide ghosts. Unknown to naive human onlookers, these "miracles" are purely strategic. They're part of a plot. The hidden intent of these miracle-workers is to deceive and destroy. Paul warned about:

> ...*the working of Satan, with **all power, signs, and lying wonders,** and with all unrighteous deception among those who perish, because they did not receive the love of the truth, that they might be saved. And for this reason God will send them strong delusion, that they should believe the lie, that they all may be condemned who did not believe the truth but had pleasure in unrighteousness* (2 Thessalonians 2:9-10, emphasis added).

People may be "hungry for signs," but above all, *they need the truth.* Paul wrote that those who "receive the love of the truth" will be "saved." Let me clarify: I'm not against all miracles, for God certainly can, has, does, and will perform mighty and wonderful works. But we need spiritual discernment to detect the true nature of the performer. The Bible tells us that both God and the devil can perform signs. The Lord performed awesome miracles when He delivered Israel out of Egypt in the time of Moses. God sent ten plagues and revealed His power. But now notice: "Pharaoh also called the wise men and the sorcerers...[and] *they also did in like manner with their enchantments*" (Exod. 7:11, emphasis added). Thus Pharaoh's magicians also performed miracles. The lesson for us is that miracles themselves are not unquestionable proof of heavenly origin. The key factor is what ideas are being taught. Remember, Isaiah wrote, "If they *speak* not according to this word, it is because there is no light in them" (Isa. 8:20, emphasis added). It's not *the act*, but *the doctrine* that establishes genuineness. If the message is, "Hi honey, it's me, your dead husband!" then we can know it's a demon. According to the Bible, "Dead men don't tell tales."

Let's return to preparations for the battle of Armageddon. God's Word predicts, "For they are spirits of demons, performing signs, which *go out* to the kings of the earth and of the whole world, to gather them to the battle of that great day of God Almighty" (Rev. 16:14, emphasis added). In this verse the Bible is alerting the entire human family that there will be an end-of-the-age apocalyptic burst of the demonic immediately preceding earth's last conflict. Demons will *"go out"* as never before. It will seem like the very gates of hell have been opened. Legions of pent-up forces will be unleashed from the abyss.

This infernal army will target *"the kings* of the earth and the whole world." "Kings" in prophecy often refer, not simply to individual rulers, but to entire kingdoms or nations. The Book of Daniel, which parallels much of Revelation, makes this clear. One dark night Daniel dreamed of "four great beasts" (Dan. 7:3). Before dawn, a holy angel explained, "These great beasts, which are four, are four kings, which shall arise out of the earth" (Dan. 7:17 KJV). Thus the four "beasts" represented "four kings." Then the angel further clarified: "The fourth beast shall be a fourth kingdom on earth" (Dan. 7:23). Put the pieces together. A "beast" represents a king *and his kingdom.* So when Revelation 16:14 says that "spirits of demons" will "go out to the kings of the earth and the whole world," this is a prediction of unprecedented, global activity. Satan's legions will spread all over planet Earth, targeting continents, countries, nations, governments, cities, and villages everywhere.

Performing signs and wonders, disguising their true identities, and lying through their devilish teeth, the apocalyptic goal of these demonic forces is "to gather" all nations "to the battle of that great day of God Almighty." *"To gather"* means to bring separate parts together into one. The Bible mentions gatherings frequently, often in reference to the gathering of crops for harvest. Jesus

Christ spoke of gatherings in His parables. Below are two parables of deep significance.

And His disciples came to Him, saying, "Explain to us the parable of the tares of the field." He answered and said to them: "He who sows the good seed is the Son of Man. The field is the world, the good seeds are the sons of the kingdom, but the tares are the sons of the wicked one. The enemy who sowed them is the devil, the harvest is the end of the age, and the reapers are the angels. ***Therefore as the tares are gathered and burned in the fire, so it will be at the end of this age.*** *The Son of Man will send out His angels, and they will gather out of His kingdom all things that offend, and those who practice lawlessness, and will cast them into the furnace of fire. There will be wailing and gnashing of teeth. Then the righteous will shine forth as the sun in the kingdom of their Father. He who has ears to hear, let him hear!"* (Matthew 13:36-43, emphasis added).

"Again, the kingdom of heaven is like a dragnet that was cast into the sea and gathered some of every kind, which, when it was full, they drew to shore; ***and they sat down and gathered the good into vessels,*** *but threw the bad away.* ***So it will be at the end of the age.*** *The angels will come forth, separate the wicked from among the just, and cast them into the furnace of fire. There will be wailing and gnashing of teeth"* (Matthew 13:47-50, emphasis added).

Both parables have apocalyptic contexts. Both apply to "the end of the age." In His first parable, the heavenly storyteller compares finally lost souls to noxious weeds that are eventually "gathered" and "burned in the fire." In His second one, He likens His blood-bought children, "the just," to good fish that are "gathered" by holy angels into "vessels." When Revelation says, "They are spirits of demons, performing signs, which go out to the kings of the earth and of the whole world, *to gather them to the battle of that great day of God Almighty*" (Rev. 16:14)—this is an apocalyptic prediction of a final gathering of deluded human beings into one last devilish trap at the culmination of earth's history. The gatherers are demonic spirits. Those gathered are unfortunate sinners throughout the "whole world" who fail to discern the snare.

The deluded ones are gathered "to the *battle* of that great day of God Almighty." The word "*battle*" implies combat between opposing armies; and in Revelation, this is surely the case. This conflict goes far beyond earthly commanders, military troops, rolling tanks, heat-seeking missiles, or nuclear bombs. Essentially, it's a spiritual conflict. Listed on the side of the enemy are "the dragon," "the beast," "the false prophet," "great Babylon," "spirits of demons," and "the kings [nations] of the earth and of the whole world" (Rev. 16:13,19,14). This apocalyptic conglomeration represents the combined forces of satanic delusion all over planet Earth at "the end of the age."

The commander and chief of this macabre army is lucifer himself. "The battle" to be engaged is the closing phase of the Great War that initially commenced beyond the stars. In the heavenly courts, "Michael and his angels fought with the dragon; and the dragon and his angels fought, but they did not prevail, nor was a place found for them in heaven any longer" (Rev. 12:7). In that first engagement, the devil's soldiers were angelic; but in the final battle, his ranks have increased dramatically. Now he commands not only fallen angels, but fallen men. Now the "whole world" has joined his side. Humanity itself has become imbued with "spirits of demons" and become, as it were, his "Special Ops Forces." Behind the scenes, satan orchestrates, coordinates, manipulates, and controls. The clock is about to strike twelve. It's almost time for the Mother of all Battles—"the battle of the great day of God Almighty...Armageddon" (Rev. 16:14,16).

A careful study of Revelation chapter 16 reveals that the battle of Armageddon is not a mere military conflict centered in a tiny valley north of Jerusalem against Jews, as is commonly understood. Instead, it's a global clash between the totality of lucifer's forces and "*God Almighty.*" Weapons, bullets, and Israelis are not its focal point. Rather, God Himself is the center of the storm. Don't be fooled about this. God's character, His love, His law, His truth, His principles, and His magnificent plan to redeem sinners through the death, burial, and resurrection of His only begotten Son—*these are the core issues.* Amazingly, we can discover all of this by reading (and understanding) one Bible verse! Notice carefully,

> "*Behold, I am coming as a thief. Blessed is he who watches, and keeps his garments, lest he walk naked and they see his shame.*" *And they gathered them together to the place called in Hebrew,* **Armageddon** (Revelation 16:15-16, emphasis added).

That one verse is Revelation 16:15. As we've seen, verse 16 is the only place in the Bible where the word "Armageddon" is mentioned, and verse 15 is the only place that specifically tells us how to prepare for it. Revelation 16:15 is a key text that contains a direct message from the lips of Jesus Christ Himself. In verse 15, our Lord speaks, warns, and gives counsel. Jesus has our best interest at heart. Oh, how He loves us! Nail scars on His hands and feet are the proof. Let's analyze His instruction carefully.

"*Behold...*" This means stop, sit up, and take notice. "*I am coming...*" Jesus is coming back to earth! He will return at Armageddon. When He comes, the entire human race will be divided into two great groups. Each of us will be *with* Him, or *against* Him; on His side, or joined to His enemy. "I am coming *as a thief.*" His return will be as unexpected to the masses of men and women as the arrival of a midnight robber. The majority doesn't believe in Him. They haven't embraced the Good News of His death, burial, and resurrection from the dead in their behalf. Tragically, millions are imbibing fables, instead of biblical truth. When the Lord returns like a thief, reality hits like a two-by-four. They weren't anticipating this. Ready or not, He who "was dead" but is "alive forevermore" will descend from the skies, defeat His enemies, and rescue His faithful people.

"Blessed is he..." Jesus begins to get specific about how to be ready for Armageddon. First, a special *blessing* is pronounced on those who heed His counsel. Second, He speaks to us as individuals. Salvation is a personal matter between each of us and God alone. We aren't saved in groups. This applies to Jews, Gentiles, and Church denominations. Many find security in their church affiliation, or in their pastor, or in their church leaders. But no fallen human being can save us—neither can we save ourselves. In Revelation 16:15, our Redeemer earnestly seeks to burst this false security bubble. "Blessed *is he...*" Jesus inserted. The word "he" means you.

"Blessed is he who *watches...*" Watching is essential to our preparation to stand at Armageddon. What should we be watching? "Ghost Whisperer", "Medium", *White Noise, The Sixth Sense, Harry Potter,* "Supernatural", or other Hollywood productions about talking to dead people? No, this is not what Jesus meant. He was talking about watching for the signs of His return. "Watch and pray," Jesus urged His drowsy disciples the night before His crucifixion, "lest you enter into temptation" (Matt. 26:41). Thus to "watch" also means to watch out for "temptation," which comes from "the devil" (see Matt. 4:1-11). Satan is "the tempter" (Matt. 4:3). Those who imagine, as Sylvia Browne confesses, that there is "no fear, no guilt, no sin, no hell, and no Satan" are going to have a hard time watching out for the attacks of someone they think doesn't exist! What if American soldiers in Baghdad stopped believing that Al-Qaeda exists? Would that be smart? They'd be sitting ducks for snipers, suicide bombers, and mines. How can you watch out for someone you think isn't there?

"Blessed is he who watches, and *keeps his garments...*" Believe it or not, these three words—"keeps his garments"—contain the heart of this book. We've talked about "garments" before remember? In this passage, Jesus Christ is referring to the spotless white robe of His own perfect righteousness—not our own righteousness (see Phil. 3:9)—that He is now mercifully offering to sinners to replace their sins. This special clothing is mentioned many times in the Apocalypse (see Rev. 7:9, 13; 19:8). Notice our Savior's personal appeal to each of us in Revelation chapter 3:

> *I counsel you to buy from Me gold refined in the fire, that you may be rich; and **white garments,** that you may be clothed, that the shame of your nakedness may not be revealed; and anoint your eyes with eye salve, that you may see* (Revelation 3:18, emphasis added).

In Revelation 16:15—the verse right before "Armageddon" is mentioned—Jesus Christ identifies the wearing of these "white garments" as the golden key to being prepared for the battle of God Almighty. The entire verse reads, *"Behold, I am coming as a thief. Blessed is he who watches, and keeps his garments, lest he walk naked and they see his shame."*

This verse takes us full circle—right back to Genesis. Jesus Christ's how-to-prepare-for-Armageddon counsel is rooted in what first occurred in Paradise. The first human beings to "walk naked" were Adam and Eve in the Garden of Eden. They felt "shame" because they obeyed the snake. Here's the Scripture account:

> *So when the woman saw that the tree was good for food, that it was pleasant to the eyes, and a tree desirable to make one wise, she took of its fruit and ate. She also gave to her husband with her, and he ate. Then the eyes of both of them were opened, **and they knew that they were naked;** and they sewed fig leaves together and made themselves coverings. And they heard the sound of the Lord God walking in the garden in the cool of the day, and Adam and his wife hid themselves from the presence of the Lord God among the trees of the garden. Then the Lord God called to Adam and said to him, "Where are you?" So he said, "I heard Your voice*

in the garden, and I was afraid because I was naked; and I hid myself" (Genesis 3:6-10, emphasis added).

Adam and Eve experienced nakedness because they believed the serpent's lie, "You will not surely die," and ate the forbidden fruit. "For dust you are, and to dust you shall return," was God Almighty's prompt reply. These fearful words must have echoed and reechoed inside their guilty heads. But they were not left without hope. As we've already seen, "the Lord God made *tunics of skin, and clothed them*" (Gen. 3:21, emphasis added). A new command was issued to slay an animal. Blood spattered, coats of skins were woven, and fig leaves were laid aside. Then the Lord placed over their naked bodies an entirely new set of clothes. "I'm wearing the skin of a dead animal," Adam may have said to Eve. "Me too," his wife might have replied. *There must be a reason*, they probably thought. There was. But neither Adam nor Eve ever fully comprehended it. It wasn't just to keep them warm, or modest, although this was important. The primary reason was spiritual. *Those garments represented the perfect righteousness of a loving Savior who would someday die for their sins, and then rise from the dead.*

Adam and Eve were originally created with perfect bodies. But after they sinned, the aging process slowly took its toll. Adam's strong, agile body lost it elasticity. His back ached. His vision faded. Eve lost her figure as her hair turned gray. In time, her teeth probably fell out. Adam may have ended up bald. Finally, death overtook them both. The Bible records:

So all the days that Adam lived were nine hundred and thirty years; **and he died** (Genesis 5:5, emphasis added).

This proves that God was right, and that the serpent was wrong. The Lord's "to dust you shall return" pronouncement was verified. Funeral services were probably held for both Adam and Eve. Eulogies may have been read, and memories relived. Sons, daughters, and friends undoubtedly shed tears.

Final good-byes were spoken. Two holes were dug in the ground. Then the cold, lifeless bodies of the first man and woman ever created were laid in the earth. "*And he died*," the inspired text tells us.

Is that it?—Two funerals, two graves, and decaying bodies to be digested by worms? Secular humanists think this is the end; but thankfully, the Lord doesn't agree with their dismal assessment. According to God's Book, death is not the end. But the truth must be told. Yes, there is hope, *but only one hope.* Paul wrote, "For since by man came death, *by Man also came the resurrection of the dead*" (1 Cor. 15:21, emphasis added). That "Man" is Jesus Christ, the Son of God. One unique Sunday morning, beside an empty tomb, a holy angel announced to a group of astonished women:

> "*Do not be afraid, for I know that you seek Jesus who was crucified. He is not here; for **He is risen**, as He said. Come, see the place where the Lord lay. And go quickly and tell His disciples that **He is risen from the dead,** and indeed He is going before you into Galilee; there you will see Him. Behold, I have told you.*" So they went out quickly from the tomb with fear and great joy, and ran to bring His disciples word" (Matthew 28:5-8, emphasis added).

The life, death, burial, and resurrection of Jesus Christ from the dead contain humanity's only hope. It was the hope of Adam and Eve; and it is our hope today. This is the central truth of the Bible, around which all other truths cluster. When Jesus walked this earth, He resisted the fiercest assaults of He ancient enemy who first possessed a snake in Eden. Our Savior overcame every temptation, developed a perfect "robe" (character) of righteousness in our behalf, died on the cross for our sins, and then—praise Him!—He was raised to life. *This alone* is what makes it legally possible for a Holy God to pardon repentant sinners and to place "white garments" over our spiritual nakedness. *Get it?* Has the light come on? Do you realize the importance of what you are reading? The white robe! The white robe! Without it, we're lost.

Now let's go back to Revelation chapter 16 and notice again what Heaven's Conqueror said:

> *"Behold, I am coming as a thief. Blessed is he who watches, and **keeps his garments, lest he walk naked and they see his shame.**" And they gathered them together to the place called in Hebrew, Armageddon* (Revelation 16:15-16, emphasis added).

Without those "garments," we'll end up naked at Armageddon. Now you know that Jesus is not talking about blue jeans, sports jackets, T-shirts, or Nike tennis shoes. And being "naked" doesn't mean having one's belly button exposed (although God's true saints will exemplify Christian modesty in public). Our Lord is warning about *spiritual nakedness*, which means to be caught in a state of sin and exposed to the just judgment of a Holy God without a covering. This was Adam and Eve's plight after they listened to the snake. There they stood—guilty, exposed, condemned. Then God covered them. In Revelation 16:15, Jesus Christ plainly warned that every person who remains uncovered, or who thinks he is just fine without "his garments" (the "white" ones), will inevitably "walk naked." Even worse, others will *"see his shame."* This means that their sins and guilt will be exposed before men and angels at Armageddon. What a solemn thought!

The bottom line is that unless we are individually "covered" with the heavenly "garments" of Jesus Christ's spotless righteousness—which is synonymous for being forgiven for our sins—we're damned and doomed. Whether we like it or not, this is the message of God's Book. Everything started in Genesis, and it all winds up in Revelation. There's no way around this. God is holy, sin is sin, sin merits the death penalty, and Jesus Christ is our only hope. May our hearts be deeply impressed by these inspired verses:

> *For **all have sinned** and fall short of the glory of God"* (Romans 3:23, emphasis added).

For the wages of sin is death, but the gift of God is eternal life in Christ Jesus our Lord" (Romans 6:23, emphasis added).

For God so loved the world that He gave His only begotten Son, *that whoever believes in Him should not perish but have everlasting life* (John 3:16, emphasis added).

For I delivered to you first of all that which I also received: that **Christ died for our sins** according to the Scriptures, and that He was buried, and that He rose again the third day according to the Scriptures (1 Corinthians 15:3-4, emphasis added).

I tell you, no; but **unless you repent** you will all likewise perish (Luke 13:3, emphasis added).

And this is the testimony: that God has given us eternal life, and this life is in His Son. **He who has the Son has life;** he who does not have the Son of God does not have life (1 John 5:11-12, emphasis added).

Here is the plain message of the above Bible texts:

1. All have sinned, all are guilty, and all are under the death sentence.

2. God so loved the world that He gave His Son to be our Savior.

3. Jesus Christ, God's Son, bore our sins, took our place, died our death, rested in Joseph's tomb, and rose from the dead.

4. We must repent of our sins and trust in the merits of Jesus Christ totally.

5. "Everlasting life" comes through Jesus alone. *It is not something we naturally possess.*

If we don't repent of our sins and trust in Jesus Christ for forgiveness, then we will be held accountable for our past, stand guilty in God's sight, remain under the death sentence, and are exposed to Heaven's justice. God is not being harsh or unfair with us, but only just. He loves us and has provided a way out. The escape route is His Son. Jesus saves, if we let Him. Those who think they are good enough *naturally*, that they have "eternal life" *naturally*, that they are going to Heaven *naturally*, are essentially depending on fig leaves. Their hope is in *self*, not God. Revelation 16:15 contains our Redeemer's earnest attempt to open our eyes, penetrate our hearts, and to lead us into the safety zone—His white robe. He hates to think of us walking naked, or being ashamed. That's why He descended from Heaven, became a helpless baby in Bethlehem, lived, suffered, died, and rose from the dead in our behalf. Jesus Himself has become our safety zone.

Let's tie this in with the theme of this book—talking to the dead. Here are four reasons why necromancy is so dangerous:

1. Every ghost who claims to be the spirit of a dead person is really a demon in disguise.

2. All communication with these impersonating spirits makes it easier for them to enter human hearts, which can lead to full demonic possession.

3. Necromancy results in believing lies, for demons are liars. Once they have gained people's confidence, they start teaching ideas insidiously designed to convince sinners that they are perfectly fine without Jesus Christ and His white robe. The popular "I'm Okay; You're Okay" philosophy *originated with demons.*

4. Sinners are led to feel secure in their sins, feel no need of repentance, become hopelessly entangled in delusion, and remain "naked" in the sight of a Holy God without a covering. The end

result is that when they die, they go down to the grave relying on themselves instead of on Jesus Christ and His resurrection from the dead—their only hope. Thus they are lost forever, and are doomed to eventually hear these fearful words from the lips of a rejected Savior, "Depart from Me, you cursed, into the everlasting fire prepared for the devil and his angels" (Matt. 25:41).

Aren't these good enough reasons to avoid talking to dead people?

A perfect example of demonic trickery is the teachings of "Seth"—the spirit who spoke to and possessed Jane Roberts. It is not difficult to uncover Seth's teachings, for they are easily accessible on countless Web sites. This is just a tiny window into Seth's insidious doctrines:

Seth: "You create your own reality."[2]

Seth: "You will reincarnate whether or not you believe that you will"[3]

Seth: "Illness and suffering are not thrust upon you by God, or by All That Is, or *by an outside agency*. They are by-products of the learning process, created by you, in themselves quite neutral..."[4]

Seth: "Your dead relatives survive."[5]

Seth: "You must realize that you are one with All That Is, and *within you* is the only one who can give blessing, and you must be willing to accept the blessing that *only you* can give, and the joy that *only you* can give to yourselves and to one another.[6]

Seth: "There should never be a word in any language that means repentance. There should only be a word that means, I bless; for when you bless, you do not need to repent...there is nothing to repent.[7]

I don't want to expose your mind—or mine—to too many "doctrines of demons" (1 Tim. 4:1), so I won't list any more of Seth's insidious ramblings. This should be enough to make my point. If you look closely at Seth's teachings, you will discover that they are essentially identical to those taught by the snake in Eden. The serpent said, "You will not surely die," and so did Seth when he taught reincarnation, and by his announcement that "Your dead relatives survive." The snake said, "You will be like God," and so did Seth when he declared, "You must realize that you are one with All That Is," and, "You create your own reality."

We don't die, and we are God—*this is Seth's doctrine*. This is the doctrine of spirits who impersonate dead people. It is also the fundamental doctrine of ancient and modern spiritualism. Not only did these ideas first lead man into sin, but they keep sinners in sin today because they lead away from Jesus Christ and from a firm reliance on His resurrection from the dead. Seth's line, "You do not need to repent," speaks for itself. What about his contention that "Illness and suffering are not thrust upon you by God...*or by an outside agency*"? This implies that there is no devil ultimately responsible for sin, pain, and death. Tricky devil! "There is no satan," satan himself is fond of saying. Don't believe it.

In the last book of the Bible, Jesus Christ Himself solemnly warns:

"Behold, I am coming as a thief. Blessed is he who watches, and keeps his garments, lest he walk naked and they see his shame." And they gathered them together to the place called in Hebrew, Armageddon (**Revelation 16:15-16**).

If you will but read your Bible, open your eyes, and discern, you will realize that the "spirits of demons" are now gathering people together around the world into their finely spun web of deception. History's hourglass is almost empty. Armageddon is at hand—"the great day of God Almighty" (Rev. 16:14).

Whose side are *you* on?

ENDNOTES

1. See http://www.time.com/time/magazine/print-out/0,8816,982807,00.html.

2. See http://www.sethlearningcenter.org/index.html#top.

3. Ibid.

4. Ibid, emphasis added.

5. See http://www.geocities.com/hal9000report/seth.html.

6. Ibid, emphasis added.

7. Ibid.

Chapter 12

REUNION DAY!

There'll be no dark valley when Jesus comes,
There'll be no dark valley when Jesus comes,
There'll be no dark valley when Jesus comes,
To gather His loved ones home.

There'll be songs of greeting when Jesus comes,
There'll be songs of greeting when Jesus comes,
And a joyful meeting when Jesus comes,
To gather His loved ones home.

—Christian Hymn, "There'll Be No Dark Valley"
Words by William O. Cushing (1823-1902)
Music by Ira D. Sankey (1840-1908)

Death stalks the living. It's real, strikes hard all around us, and it hurts. No matter how much we seek to avoid it, deny it, or rationalize it away, death eventually stares us all in the face. Death often comes suddenly. It severs relationships, shatters hope and dreams, and leaves people brokenhearted, empty, and alone. Grief over the loss of a loved one is often unimaginable; the pain beyond words.

This is perhaps the main reason why so many people try to make contact with their dead relatives. *I miss my wife!* A bereaved husband moans. *I wish we could talk once more!* Longings like this often lead the grieving into the arms of professional psychics and modern mediums. Unfortunately, it also ushers them into dark lairs of demons that delight in exploiting human weakness. No matter what they claim, demons don't care one iota about us. "*Yes dear, it's me,*" a devil may say with a million-dollar smile, "*Life is awesome on the Other Side!*" But it's all a trap. Demons offer false comfort, and then they start teaching doctrines that lead away from Bible truth. These invisible personalities are intelligent, and ruthless, with thousands of years of experience beneath their satanic belts. As we approach Armageddon, their goal is to ensnare the world.

The true God of the Bible, the Lord of Heaven and earth, understands our pain, sorrow, and loneliness. Although we have sinned against Him, His love for us remains unchanged. As proof of that love, He has provided a heavenly solution to the nightmare of funeral services, coffins, and tombstones. Nearly 2,000 years ago, His own Son entered humanity, was born in Bethlehem, grew up in Nazareth, experienced our struggles, felt our temptations, shared our pains, and then—at age 33—voluntarily submitted Himself to the horrors of the grave. By dying, Jesus met death head on. But death couldn't hold Him. Three days after His crucifixion, He stepped out of the tomb into heavenly sunlight. Thus Jesus beat death itself. Today, God's solution to body bags and tears is not dialogue with the deceased, but faith in the Risen One. Jesus Himself is our *Good News*. He remains untouched by demonic influences.

Most Christians wholeheartedly believe these truths; but there is something many seem to have missed. Just as our Savior died and rose from the dead, *even so shall we also rise from the dead at the end of the world.* Sadly, this fact has been largely ignored by modern Christianity, but it's as biblical as

Noah's ark, the Passover, and the Ten Commandments. Paul wrote the majority of the New Testament. Although he firmly believed in the resurrection of Jesus Christ, he also looked forward to his own resurrection. Notice his words to the Philippians:

> *That I may know Him and the power of His resurrection, and the fellowship of His sufferings, being conformed to His death, if, by any means,* **I may attain to the resurrection from the dead** (Philippians 3:10-11 emphasis added).

Paul longed to know Jesus Christ, "and the power of His resurrection." But that "power" was to be manifested, not alone through Christ's bodily exodus out of Joseph's damp tomb, but by Paul's own resurrection from the grave. "If by any means," Paul testified, "*I might attain* to the resurrection of the dead." Thus the *past* resurrection of Jesus Christ was Phase One, and Paul's own *future* resurrection was Phase Two. Paul repeated this conviction as he defended his faith before the Roman governor Felix:

> *But this I confess unto thee, that after the way which they call heresy, so worship I the God of my fathers, believing all things which are written in the law and in the prophets: And have* **hope toward God**, *which they themselves also allow,* **that there shall be a resurrection of the dead,** *both of the just and unjust* (Acts 24:14-15 KJV, emphasis added).

Although a prisoner before Felix, Paul stood unafraid. His heart was at peace because of his firm "hope toward God." What was his hope? "*That there shall be a resurrection of the dead,*" he testified. Once again, Paul firmly believed in the past resurrection of Jesus Christ. This was his anchor. But his personal hope was connected to a resurrection yet future. "*There shall be,*" Paul confessed, looking forward, "a resurrection of the dead." And Paul not only believed that he himself would be raised, but that everyone else would too! "There shall be a resurrection of the dead, *both the just and the unjust.*"

Paul's doctrine was rooted in Christ's own teaching. Throughout His public ministry, Jesus not only predicted His death and resurrection, but also a future resurrection of both the saved and the lost. In John chapter five, the Son of God majestically declared:

Marvel not at this: for the hour is coming, in the which all that are in the graves shall hear His voice, and shall come forth; they that have done good, unto the resurrection of life; and they that have done evil, unto the resurrection of damnation (John 5:28-29 KJV).

Here Jesus plainly predicted two future resurrections. "The hour is coming," He declared, when "all that are in the graves" will "hear His voice" and "come forth." What an awakening! The Risen One will speak. His voice shall pierce the ears of the dead, summoning them back to life. Those who are saved will "come forth" in "the resurrection of life," while the lost awake "to the resurrection of damnation." Two groups. Two resurrections. Both future. Solemn thought!

In John chapter six, Jesus again spoke of a future resurrection, but this time He focused exclusively on those who should believe in Him. Describing the hope of His people, Christ announced:

*This is the will of the Father who sent Me, that of all He has given Me, I should lose nothing, **but should raise it up at the last day...***

*And this is the will of Him who sent Me, that everyone who sees the Son and believes in Him may have everlasting life; **and I will raise him up at the last day...***

*No one can come to Me unless the Father who sent Me draws him; **and I will raise him up at the last day...***

*Whoever eats My flesh and drinks My blood has eternal life, **and I will raise him up at the last day*** (John 6:39, 40, 44, 54, emphasis added).

Jesus was hardly in the habit of repeating Himself for no reason. In John 6, He found a reason. He understood the work of the serpent, and the subtle activity of demons that snarled, "My name is Legion, for we are many." With a heavy heart, He also knew the illusions of mediums and spiritualists. With bitter grief, He even foresaw the confusion that would exist within much of Christianity about life, death, burial, and resurrection. So He decided to "make it plain," so that no honest heart would miss it. That's why He stated not just once, or twice, or even three times, but four times, that He would personally resurrect those who believe in Him on "the last day."

When is "the last day"? No one knows the exact date, but we do know it is a day of resurrection. "I will raise him up at the last day," Christ declared. Thus the "last day" is when believers are raised "up," which obviously means *up from their graves*. What event brings this about? The New Testament is clear that it is when Jesus Christ returns. In other words, when Jesus comes *down* from Heaven, that's when His people come up from their graves.

Although the doctrine of the return of Jesus Christ has being neglected by many within modern Christendom, this awesome event has been predicted by every New Testament writer, which includes Matthew (see Matt. 16:27), Mark (see Mark 13:26), Luke (see Luke 21:27), John (see John 14:3), Paul (see Titus 2:13), Peter (see 2 Pet. 3:10), James (see James 5:8), and Jude (see Jude 14). And these texts are only a fragment of all of the Scriptures describing the Big Day. During His public ministry, Jesus Himself declared:

For the Son of Man shall come in the glory of His Father with His angels; *and then He shall reward every man according to his works* (Matthew 16:27 KJV, emphasis added).

Then they will see the Son of Man coming in the clouds with great power and glory. And then He will send His angels, and gather together His elect from the four winds, from the farthest part of earth to the farthest part of heaven (Mark 13:26-27, emphasis added).

Reiterating what his Master taught, Paul wrote:

For the grace of God that brings salvation has appeared to all men, teaching us that, denying ungodliness and worldly lusts, we should live soberly, righteously, and godly in the present age, **looking for the blessed hope and glorious appearing of our great God and Savior Jesus Christ,** *who gave Himself for us, that He might redeem us from every lawless deed and purify for Himself His own special people, zealous for good works* (Titus 2:11-14, emphasis added).

In Titus 2:13 Paul called the return of Jesus Christ "the blessed hope," and said that every true Christian should be "*looking for*" this climactic event. Our world is a vast lazar house filled with problems. On every hand we see heartache, pain, sickness, and death. Islamic terrorism, natural disasters, political corruption, and tragic accidents are daily reported in newspapers, on the Internet, and on radio and TV. Pornography, child abuse, poverty, and divorce are rampant. In the midst of social turmoil and global chaos, the cries of suffering humanity daily ascend to the King of Kings. There's only one solution to this world's woes. Political processes can't implement it. It goes beyond judicial legislation. Neither Republicans nor Democrats can vote it in. It's coming down from the sky:

For as the lightning comes from the east and flashes to the west, **so also will the coming of the Son of Man be** (Matthew 24:27, emphasis added).

This is the hope of the Church! Shortly before His crucifixion, Jesus comforted His followers by pointing their troubled minds to His future return. How we need Christ's words today! The Savior declared:

> *Let not your heart be troubled; you believe in God, believe also in Me. In My Father's house are many mansions; if it were not so, I would have told you. I go to prepare a place for you. And if I go and prepare a place for you,* **I will come again and receive you to Myself;** *that where I am, there you may be also"* (John 14:1-3, emphasis added).

There it is in black and white. We need not fear. "*I will come again,*" Jesus promised. Almost everyone admits He was here once. Even those who don't believe He was the Son of God acknowledge that a historical person named Jesus Christ was born in Bethlehem, grew up in rural Nazareth, taught in the streets of Jerusalem, was rejected by the Jewish Sanhedrin, was tried by Pontius Pilate, whipped by Roman soldiers, and then nailed to a tree. *The primary controversy swirls around His resurrection.* Did Jesus really rise from the dead? "Definitely!" declares the New Testament; and it also affirms Christ's announcement, "*I will come again.*" Now don't miss what Jesus said next— "*and receive you to Myself;* that where I am, there you may be also." The Master Himself said it. When will He "receive" us to Himself? When He "comes again"! How is this possible? There's only one answer. *By resurrecting His people from the dead.*

One of the clearest Bible chapters linking the return of Jesus Christ with the resurrection of God's saints is First Corinthians chapter 15, written by Paul. Let's examine this section carefully, starting with verses 20-23. First I will quote Paul's words, and then add my comments:

> *But now Christ is risen from the dead, and has become the firstfruits of those who have fallen asleep* (1 Corinthians 15:20).

In verse 20, Paul acknowledges the resurrection of Jesus Christ and calls Jesus "the firstfruits" of those who have "fallen asleep," or died. Thus the resurrection of Christ comes first, and this will be followed by the future resurrection of God's saints.

For since by man came death, by Man also came the resurrection of the dead (1 Corinthians 15:21).

Death started with the first created man. Adam sinned, and as a consequence, "he died" (Gen. 5:5). Jesus Christ, who is often called "the Second Adam," undid this disaster by offering up His life, and then by being resurrected from the dead.

For as in Adam all die, even so in Christ all shall be made alive (1 Corinthians 15:22).

Because he was the first created human being, Adam was a representative man. His disobedience affected us all. Because of his sin, we "all die." But by virtue of Jesus Christ's sinless life, atoning sacrifice for our sins, and resurrection from the dead, He has become the new head of the human family. Because of what Jesus has accomplished, eventually, *"all shall be made alive."* This means that every human being who has ever been born, lived and died throughout history shall one day be "made alive," or resurrected from the dead!

But each one in his own order: Christ the firstfruits, afterward those who are Christ's at His coming (1 Corinthians 15:23).

There is a divine "order," or sequence, to Heaven's plan. First, there was the resurrection of Jesus Christ nearly 2,000 years ago. Then "afterward, those who are Christ's *at His coming.*" Thus Paul shifts from Christ's resurrection to the resurrection of God's saints, which will occur "at His coming."

The climax of Paul's discourse comes at the end of First Corinthians chapter 15. With a hope fully established by the resurrection of Jesus Christ in the past, and with his eye on the horizon, the man who wrote the majority of the New Testament declared:

Now this I say, brethren, that flesh and blood cannot inherit the kingdom of God; nor does corruption inherit incorruption (1 Corinthians 15:50).

Because Adam sinned, our bodies are now composed of fallen "flesh and blood." In this sinful, mortal, decaying state, we "cannot inherit the kingdom of God." A change is needed. Our innate "corruption" must be replaced by "incorruption."

Behold, I tell you a mystery: We shall not all sleep, but we shall all be changed—(1 Corinthians 15:51).

The details of this transition are God's "mystery." Puny human minds cannot comprehend the Lord's science. Yet such a feat is not difficult for the Almighty, who first formed man from the dust of the earth. "We shall not all sleep," or die, declared the apostle. When Jesus returns, there will be two distinct classes of the saved. First, there will be those who "sleep," or who have already died. Second, there will be those who will be living, eyewitnesses of Christ's Second Coming. Paul mentions both groups. Whether dead or alive, "we shall all be changed."

In a moment, in the twinkling of an eye, at the last trumpet. For the trumpet will sound, and the dead will be raised incorruptible, and we shall be changed (1 Corinthians 15:52).

In a flash, quicker than you can blink, both groups will be "changed" instantaneously, in a "moment" of time. This transformation occurs at "the last trumpet," which means at the very end of the world. "For the trumpet will *sound*." Trumpets are loud, not silent. The return of Jesus Christ will be highly audible. It will be heard in America, Russia, China, Africa, Australia, and on every island on the sea—all over the world. Everyone will hear it, even those who forgot to put in their hearing aids that day. When God's heavenly trumpet blasts, "the dead will be raised." This is the glorious resurrection of God's saints!

For long ages the people of God have been among "the dead," but at the Second Coming they will be "raised" back to life. They rise out of their graves "incorruptible," which means they are given new bodies bearing no trace of the effects of sin. "And we shall be changed." Those who witness the Second Coming will be given new bodies also. O happy day! No more arthritis, back pains, gray hair, false teeth, contact lenses, or embarrassment over one's sagging figure. Ladies, won't that be nice? Health insurance will be history; Medicare, a thing of the past. No one will ever again dial 911. No more ambulance sirens or paramedics. Hospitals will go out of business. No plastic surgeon can duplicate the Lord's touch. God's resurrected people will be like Adam and Eve before the fall. They will have perfect bodies!

For this corruptible must put on incorruption, and this mortal must put on immortality (1 Corinthians 15:53).

As we saw earlier, today we are "mortal," or subject to death. Such is the sad consequence of eating the forbidden fruit. Holy angels with flaming swords made sure that mortality remained the condition of every descendant of Adam and Eve. But when Jesus returns, this unfortunate state is reversed. Finally, after thousands of years of painful history where human beings have lost their strength, their vision, their teeth, shrunk in size, stooped over, shriveled up, suffered, died, decayed, and become food for worms, it is time for "this mortal" to "put on immortality." Hallelujah! Shouldn't Christians be writing, talking, teaching, preaching, and broadcasting more about the importance of Resurrection Day? Shouldn't it receive greater attention from our nation's pulpits? It even merits prime-time coverage on the Nightly News.

So when this corruptible has put on incorruption, and this mortal has put on immortality, then shall be brought to pass the saying that is written: "Death is swallowed up in victory" (1 Corinthians 15:54).

The last part of verse 54 is a direct quote from the Old Testament. Sometime around 700 B.C., the prophet Isaiah predicted that the Lord of life would someday "swallow up death forever" (Isa. 25:8); but that time has tarried for many, many years. But no longer! *"Then,"* Paul wrote, referring to Resurrection Day, "shall be brought to pass the saying that is written: Death is swallowed up in victory." The day has finally arrived for death to be vanquished. And amazingly, this time, *God's weapon is His saints!* Patches of dust join together. Disintegrated hearts miraculously start beating again. Brains begin functioning. Eyes open. Tombstones crack worldwide as hands beneath "Rest in Peace" epitaphs emerge amidst rocks and dirt. Shining faces appear, never again to cough their last breath. God's Word will be fulfilled, "Death is swallowed up in victory."

"O Death, where is your sting? O Hades [grave], *where is your victory?"* (1 Corinthians 15:55).

Resurrected saints will repeat these exact words as they rise from their graves. Now let me ask you: Why would God's people be so thrilled about conquering death *if there was no death*? Why the shout of triumph? The answer is obvious. Because death is horribly real, no matter what psychics and mediums tell us. Ask Adam and Eve. Ask Moses. Ask almost anyone lying helplessly on his or her deathbed. If death wasn't real, why weep at funeral services? Why visit gravesides? Why lay flowers beside tombstones? Although so many have mentally accepted the serpent's doctrine ("You will not surely die"), reality works hard to counteract this error. Of course death is real. Like a scorpion, its "sting" is venomous. But praise God! Because of Jesus Christ's triumphant resurrection, the victory of believers is certain. On Resurrection Morning, both death and the grave experience a crushing defeat as unnumbered millions rise from the earth shouting, "*O Death, where is your sting? O Hades* [grave]*, where is your victory?*" An old saint on his deathbed testified,

> If you miss me, don't dismay,
> I may have to rest in a mound of clay,
> But when I hear the trumpet sound,
> I'm coming out of the cold, cold ground!

How utterly fantastic! Now you know the message of First Corinthians 15! Before this book concludes, we must also examine First Thessalonians 4:13-18. In this final section, Paul repeats the same encouraging truths recorded in First Corinthians 15, but adds more details, especially about seeing our dead relatives again. Follow me closely.

> *But I do not want you to be ignorant, brethren, concerning those who have fallen asleep, lest you sorrow as others who have no hope* (1 Thessalonians 4:13).

Paul wrote First Thessalonians to a group of new Christians in the Greek city of Thessalonica. At the time of his writing, some of the believers had recently died. The remaining saints were confused about this. What would happen to their deceased relatives and friends? *Will we ever see them again?* those early believers wondered. So Paul addressed the issue. First and foremost, he didn't want them to be "ignorant." Have you heard the line, "What you don't know can't hurt you"? It's not true. Ignorance can be deadly, especially if a ghost appears in your bedroom and you think it's your dead mother.

Paul sought to enlighten his converts about "those who have *fallen asleep.*" Here again, as in First Corinthians 15, Paul wrote that dying is like going to sleep. This is a common Bible teaching (see Ps. 13:3; Dan. 12:3; John 11:11-14;

Acts 7:60; 1 Cor. 15:6; etc.). Although their beloved dead had "fallen asleep," Paul encouraged the living believers not to "sorrow as others who have no hope." Now notice, Paul didn't say, "Don't sorrow." He was under no illusions about death's bitter reality. He knew death brings grief and pain; but he told the Thessalonians not to "sorrow *as others* who have *no hope.*" For Paul, there was hope! What was that hope? You already know the answer—*the resurrection of the dead.* Paul continued:

> *For if we believe that Jesus died and rose again, even so God will bring with Him those who sleep in Jesus* (1 Thessalonians 4:14).

This verse is a bit tricky, but a careful reading of text will solve any problems. Paul begins with the fundamental fact that "Jesus died and rose again." Don't forget this, for it forms the basis of his entire argument. "Jesus died," was buried in Joseph's tomb, *but then God brought Him up from the dead.* "Even so," Paul wrote, which means in like manner, "God will bring with Him those who sleep in Jesus." In other words, just as God brought His Son *up* from the grave, "even so" will He bring *up* from their graves "those who sleep in Jesus." It's that simple.

Let's return to this "sleep" idea, but now let's connect it with talking to dead people. In verse 13, Paul wrote that the Thessalonian dead had "fallen asleep." In verse 14, he called those same dead Thessalonians "those who sleep in Jesus." Now think about it. Is it possible to carry on an intelligent conversation with a sleeping person? Try it sometime. Our son Seth is 28 months old. Though just a little guy, he's a real chatterbox. Seth talks to my wife Kristin and me, and we talk back. *But not when he's asleep.* When Seth takes a nap or goes to bed for the night, there's no conversation at all. It's impossible to converse with sleeping people!

Paul understood this. Even though the Thessalonians were heartbroken and confused about their beloved dead, Paul *never* would have encouraged them to attend a Jerusalem séance, or a Thessalonian séance, or any other séance. First of all, he knew what Moses had written about mediums and spiritists; and second, he understood the impossibility of conversing with sleeping saints. Paul longed to comfort his friends, but he didn't do it by encouraging communication with ghosts. Instead of pushing his converts into the arms of demonic impersonators, Paul offered another hope entirely—a biblical hope—the resurrection of the dead.

> *For this we say to you by the word of the Lord, that we who are alive and remain until the coming of the Lord will by no means precede those who are asleep* (1 Thessalonians 4:15).

Instead of quoting psychic experts, metaphysical gurus, or even religious scholars, Paul taught "the word of the Lord." He understood that the Bible is our safeguard, and that truth alone can protect us from devils. Continuing on, Paul identified two groups: "we who are alive" and "those who are asleep." Obviously, these two groups are quite different. One group is living; the other, dead. Look carefully. Those "who are alive and remain until the coming of the Lord *will by no means precede* those who are asleep." Did you catch that? Paul declared that the living won't "precede," or go ahead of, the dead, neither will the dead go ahead of the living. In other words, *both groups will enter God's kingdom together.* When?

At "the coming of the Lord" (verse 15)!

> *For the Lord Himself will descend from heaven with a shout, with the voice of an archangel, and with the trumpet of God. And the dead in Christ will rise first* (1 Thessalonians 4:16).

The "Lord Himself" will return. The same Jesus who was born in Bethlehem, lived a holy life, suffered in Gethsemane, was crucified, buried, rose again from the dead, and who ascended beyond the stars; this same Jesus will "descend from heaven with a shout, with the voice of an archangel, and with the trumpet of God." His return will be loud, and visible. The blast of God's trumpet will penetrate the ears of His slumbering saints worldwide, "and the dead in Christ will rise first." Once again, it's Resurrection Day! Paul wrote: "the dead...will rise."

But notice that it is only "the dead *in Christ*" that are raised when Jesus returns. Sadly, the vast majority of deceased sinners are not in this group. When they died, they died *outside* of Christ, thus they are not resurrected when the Lord descends from heaven with a shout, voice, and trumpet. They rise at a different time—at the end of the Millennium (see Rev. 20:5a). Then they will be "judged according to their works," and finally sentenced to "the lake of fire" (see Rev. 20:5a, 11-15). Let's make sure we are among those "in Christ"!

Then we who are alive and remain shall be caught up together with them in the clouds to meet the Lord in the air. And thus we shall always be with the Lord (1 Thessalonians 4:17).

This is one of the most wonderful verses in the entire Bible. Verse 16 describes the moment when "the dead in Christ will rise." "*Then*," Paul wrote in verse 17, "we who are alive and remain shall be caught up *together* with them...." Don't miss it! One of the grandest moments in all of human history is being described. That all-important word, "*together*," depicts the joyful reunion of the living and the dead. Parents whose babies were snatched away by death will behold their sweet faces again. Husbands will embrace their wives, and wives their husbands. Fathers will rejoin their sons, and daughters will tearfully hug their mothers. Will we really recognize our deceased relatives and friends? Yes! That's exactly what "together" means! The context is the reuniting of loved ones whose intimate bonds have been ripped apart by death's cruel blow.

Recently I found myself walking through a sprawling Southern California cemetery reading epitaphs engraved on tombstones. One particular stone caught my eye:

Joseph L. Carpenter, M.D.
1941 – 1981
Beloved Husband of Irene

The following words engraved directly below this man's name touched me deeply. Surrounded by rolling hills, stately trees, and bundles of flowers placed lovingly above the silent forms of dead husbands, wives, parents, grandparents, and children, this is what I read:

Love is a golden chain death tries to break, but all in vain
To have, to hold, and then to part
Is the greatest sorrow of our hearts
We who love will learn to live with our pain
Until we are together again

"Until we are together again." Reunions like this will surely occur! Such is the hope we have in Jesus. "Never part again," are the words of a famous Christian hymn. I can hardly wait.

But remember, according to First Thessalonians 4:13-18, *"Then"* (verse 17)—which means at the return of Jesus Christ—is when we can expect to meet our beloved dead again. This bears repeating. Paul wrote that it is when Jesus Christ returns to raise the dead that we will be "together" with our deceased relatives and friends, *and not before this.* Until then, all communication with the dead is forbidden, séances are taboo, and mediumship is categorically condemned. Let me say it one more time: As a solace for our grief, the Bible points us to the return of Jesus Christ and Resurrection Day, not spooky conversations with the Other Side. This is the message of Scripture. This is the doctrine of Paul. This is the truth of God's Word.

Additionally—and this is important to realize—according to the inspired text, only those *in Christ* will participate in this reunion. Remember, in verse 13, Paul spoke of all "others who have *no hope.*" The solemn reality is that those who cling to their fig leaf garments, who reject Jesus Christ's death and resurrection in their behalf, who despise His gracious offer of a "white robe," and who refuse to repent of their sins—these have no real, true, biblical hope of either eternal salvation or of being reunited with those they have sorrowfully laid to rest. And to offer such hope outside of Christ is a scam, which is exactly what demons are so adept at doing. "Be happy," a ghost may say. "I'll see you soon on the Other Side!" But this is a deadly delusion. "No fear, no guilt, no sin, no hell, and no Satan" is actually a message that originates from satan, keeps sinners in sin, can't remove guilt, and leads to ruin. All such communications come from demons in disguise.

"Then we who are alive and remain shall be caught up together with them *in the clouds....*" On that grand day, God's resurrected and translated saints will ascend upward, away from this lost world, with its darkness, delusions, and devils. We'll soar into the clouds! But beyond reunion with loved ones, and a free space ride, the happiest part of all will be *"to meet the Lord* in the air" (verse 17). Of course we long to meet close companions snatched away by death. Such longings are human, and God-given. But ah...to *meet our Savior,* this will be our greatest joy. Oh to behold His smiling face! To look upon the One who endured such agony because of our sins, felt forsaken by His Father, sacrificed His life, submitted to death's grip, yet who opened death's door by rising from the grave, this will be our pinnacle of ecstasy. *"And thus we shall always be with the Lord."* Don't miss Paul's key point. *"And thus,"* which means "in this way,"—because of the return of Jesus Christ and the resurrection of the dead—*"we,"* meaning all of God's people, *"shall always be with the Lord."* The truth is confirmed. We get to be with our loving Savior when He comes again.

Therefore comfort one another with these words (1 Thessalonians 4:18).

Truth has a straight edge. At times, it may appear cold and unbending, but in the final analysis, it alone can "comfort" our souls. What are *you* searching for? Do you want teachings that are "politically correct," or biblically correct? Lies may make us feel good for a season, but their end is bitter. All they can offer is false hope, deceptive promises, leading to devastating disappointment. In contrast, Paul wrote, "comfort one another with *these words*." "These words" are the words that God Himself has inspired, not human theories. Ultimately, "these words" apply to the entire Bible—a Book that reveals unprejudiced facts about creation, the serpent's first lie, the fall of man, the Edenic death sentence, Cherubim with fiery swords, familiar spirits, Jesus Christ's atoning sacrifice, His resurrection from the dead, a white robe to cover our nakedness, hidden forces propelling humanity toward Armageddon, our Lord's triumphant return, a final resurrection of both the just and the unjust, and a joyful reunion of believers separated by death at the end of the world.

"*Comfort one another with these words,*" Paul wrote.

The bottom line message of this message is love—the love of God for a lost, dying, deluded world. God created us, knows us, and loves us. Two thousand years ago, on a lonely hill outside Jerusalem, His own Holy Son suffered the full penalty for our sins. On the third day, He rose from the dead. Isn't this enough for us? Why trust human opinions, fig leaves, or demons?

Tim was 14 years old and lived out in the country with his dad and mom. "I'm leaving!" Tim shouted to his father during a heated argument, "You'll never see me again!" With that, he left. Three years later, like the prodigal son, he thought about home.

"Mom, it's me," said a shaky voice on the other end of the phone. "Three days from now I will purchase a train ticket, and at about 3:00 P.M. my train will stop at the bottom of the hill below our house. Talk to Dad. If he is willing to take me back, ask him to hang something white on our porch. When my train passes by, if I see anything white outside, I'll get off and come home. If not, I'll keep going." Then Tim hung up the phone without giving his mother a chance to speak.

Three days later Tim purchased his ticket, boarded the train, and then sat down beside a minister. "What's up, young man?" asked the pastor, sensing the boy's nervousness. With quivering lips, Tim explained everything. About four hours later the train approached the last bend before its upcoming stop at the station below Tim's house. "Mr. Minister," Tim asked the pastor, "as we wind around the next corner you will see our house on the hill. I can't bear to look, so I'm going to close my eyes. Please look for me. If you see anything white outside our house, tell me. If not, don't say anything. Then when the train stops and starts, I'll just keep going." With that, Tim shut his eyes. The pastor prayed.

Down the tracks, round the bend, the whistle blew, and the train screeched to a halt. When the pastor anxiously peered through the window beside his seat, he was shocked at what he saw. Jumping to his feet, he grabbed the boy and shouted, "Tim, look!" Tim cracked his eyelids and was astonished to see his little homestead on the hill completely covered in white! Draped over the roof, lining the porch, and lying all around the lawn were white blankets, white pillowcases, white sheets, white towels, white tablecloths, white napkins, white socks, and even white toilet paper! Tim's parents had seized everything white that they could possibly find and flung them all around their house.

The last the minister saw of 17-year-old Tim was the boy's back as he exited the train and raced as fast as his young legs could carry him, up the hill, up the stairs, through the white sheets lining the porch, through the front door, and straight into the outstretched arms of two lonely parents who would gladly have sold literally everything they owned—including the family farm—just to be reunited with their runaway son again.

Oh how they loved and missed him! Tim got the message.

Do *you* get the message? Dear reader, this is how Jesus feels about you! He did much more than sell the family farm; He endured separation from His own Eternal Father who He loved more than words can describe. Death itself crept into His blood, into His bones, and into His heart. The entire experience was an incomprehensible nightmare. Out of love for our souls, the Lord of light embraced the darkness, and yielded to its clammy grip. "It is finished!" He shouted. Then He breathed His last breath and died. But the mystery of all mysteries is that a rocky tomb couldn't hold Him. On a bright Sunday morning, He rose from the dead.

The Son of God is "alive forevermore" (Rev. 1:18)! He is now in Heaven; but He hasn't forgotten His promise to "come again" (John 14:3) and receive us to Himself. According to God's "sure word of prophecy" (2 Peter 1:19, KJV), we are living in "the last days" (2 Tim. 3:1). Soon Jesus will return. Then "the dead in Christ will rise," and we shall be caught up "together" with our loved ones into His presence, never more to part. *"And thus we shall always be with the Lord"* (1 Thess. 4:17).

Jesus Christ has a white robe, with your name on it.

It's a gift of His love.

Don't let lucifer or his demons keep you from wearing it.

The End

ADDITIONAL RESOURCES

By
Steve Wohlberg

PERILS OF TALKING TO THE DEAD
(POCKET BOOK)

If *Demons in Disguise* has enlightened you, a smaller, pocketsize edition called *Perils of Talking to the Dead* is now available for mass distribution. Cost: $0.95 each. Quantity discounts. Great for sharing!

THE ANTICHRIST CHRONICLES
(AS SEEN ON TV)

What is the truth about the antichrist? Why does the Bible say, "even now are their many antichrists" (1 John 2:18)? *The Antichrist Chronicles* is not about popular fiction, but reality. Its focus is not an imaginary Mr. Evil who shows up after we're gone, but a present antichrist that's been around for centuries and which is even now involved in global politics. Learn what the Bible teaches, not speculative theories. Perfect for prayer meetings and home Bible studies (DVD/Book).

ISRAEL IN PROPHECY
(AS SEEN ON TV)

Today literally millions of people who study Bible prophecy have their eyes fixed upon Jerusalem. Right now, all over planet Earth, Christians are talking about the modern state of Israel, a rebuilt Jewish temple, and a final battle called Armageddon involving Iran, Russia, and the Jews. What is the truth? Does the Book of Revelation *really focus* on the Middle East? *Israel in Prophecy* is eye opening, biblical, and thoroughly centered in Jesus Christ (DVD/Book).

END-TIME DELUSIONS: THE RAPTURE, THE
ANTICHRIST, ISRAEL, AND THE END OF THE WORLD
(AS SEEN ON TV)

End-Time Delusions is Steve Wohlberg's most comprehensive book on Bible prophecy. With clarity and biblical accuracy, it exposes massive errors now flooding through media and in much of today's sensational prophecy writing. This book closely examines tightly meshed yet speculative theories about the rapture, seven-year tribulation, antichrist, and the modern Jewish state. Buttressed with solid teachings from many of Christianity's most illustrious scholars, it lets the Bible speak for itself about the past, present, and future (DVD/Book). The book includes easy-to-follow study guides.

EXPOSING HARRY POTTER AND WITCHCRAFT:
THE MENACE BEHIND THE MAGIC
(AS SEEN ON TV)

The *Harry Potter* novels and movies have "mesmerized an entire generation of kids" (*Time* magazine, June 23, 2003). Most consider them harmless fiction, yet could there be a menace behind the magic? What about Wicca, a religion that practices real witchcraft and one of the fastest growing religions today? *Exposing Harry Potter and Witchcraft* is well researched, fair, and eye opening. *Learn how to protect yourself and your loved ones from dark, supernatural forces* (DVD/Book/Booklet/Tract).

ORDER LINE ONLY:
CALL TOLL FREE: 800 78-BIBLE
VISA/MASTER CARDS ACCEPTED

OR WRITE TO:
WHITE ROSE MEDIA
P.O. BOX 8057
FRESNO, CA 93747

Steve Wohlberg's solid Bible teaching is influencing people around the world.

To learn more about his growing radio and TV ministry, visit

WWW.WHITEHORSEMEDIA.COM

NOTES

_____

_____

_____

_____

_____

_____

_____

_____

_____

_____